Sigurd's Lament

Sigurd's Lament

An Alliterative Epic

by Anonymous

Discovered by Basil Augustus Peters
Translated by Wallace Walker Peters
Compiled and Edited by Hawthorne Basil Peters
Edited by Benjamin John Peters

CASCADE *Books* · Eugene, Oregon

SIGURD'S LAMENT
An Alliterative Epic

Cascade Books
An Imprint of Wipf and Stock Publishers
199 W. 8th Ave., Suite 3
Eugene, OR 97401

www.wipfandstock.com

paperback isbn: 978-1-4982-9523-9
hardcover isbn: 978-1-4982-9525-3
ebook isbn: 978-1-4982-9524-6

Cataloging-in-Publication data:

Names: Peters, Wallace Walker, translator. | Peters, Hawthorne Basil, editor

Title: Sigurd's lament : an alliterative epic / translated by Wallace Walker Peters, edited by Hawthorne Basil Peters.

Description: Eugene, OR : Imprint, 2017 | Includes bibliographical references.

Identifiers: ISBN 978-1-4982-9523-9 (paperback) | ISBN 978-1-4982-9525-3 (hardcover) | ISBN 978-1-4982-9524-6 (ebook)

Subjects: LCSH: Welsh poetry—Translations into English.

Classification: LCC PB2231 P3 2017 (print) | LCC PB2231 (electronic)

Manufactured in the U.S.A.   07/13/17

To Wallace

Come, my friends,
'Tis not too late to seek a newer world.

ALFRED, LORD TENNYSON, *ULYSSES*

Let us sit upon the ground
And tell sad stories of the death of kings.

SHAKESPEARE, *RICHARD II*

A work of art manifests in its structures a certain vision of the world.

UMBERTO ECO, *LA DEFINIZIONE DELL'ARTE*

All texts—sacred or otherwise—are constructions.

BENJAMIN JOHN PETERS, *ON THE MATTER OF TEXTS*

If the reader follows the commentary's lead beyond a certain point
she or he must realize that one is leaving the text and entering other
territory.

MICHAEL CAESAR, *UMBERTO ECO*

Contents

Preface to the First Edition

Deep in the hill country of Wales, my grandfather found an ancient scroll. My father exhausted his life translating it. I have spent mine bringing it to you. I could not have accomplished this monumental task without the help of Oxford University and the Royal British Museum. I am forever indebted to both.

As always, my wife has superseded me in love, support, and care. Without her, I am only a small man with an old book.

To my children, I only want to say that I apologize for the neglect. Someday I hope that you will understand.

If *Sigurd's Lament* is valuable, then it is only found in you, the reader. Thank you for taking the time to engage my family's work. It is nothing without you.

In the end, I look back and see little of inherent worth in this quixotic quest, but it was mine. And it brings me great pleasure to share it with you.

Hawthorne Basil Peters
London
November 24, 1980

Preface to the Second Edition

It has been twenty-nine years since I first published *Sigurd's Lament*. Who could have known the splash that it would make in either the academic community or the popular imagination? Not I.

If *Sigurd's Lament* is anything, then it is most certainly a testament to my father's belief in the written word. In the preface to the first edition, I wrote that my father exhausted his life on translating *Sigurd's Lament*. I mean just that. It drove him mad and eventually killed him. But it also gave him purpose and meaning. As far as I can tell, it has also provided countless others with the same.

Thank you, reader, for continuing to engage *Sigurd's Lament*. I am forever honored and in your debt.

Hawthorne Basil Peters
Aberdylwyth
February 1, 2009

Introduction

Sigurd's Lament is a text of great complexity. It is a poem, a treatise, and a life's work. In many ways, it is a compulsion. If you have taken it upon yourself to tackle Sigurd's Lament in its entirety, then I encourage you: leave no footnote unturned, leave no bibliographic entry unexplored, leave no stanza unread—for this text must be engaged as a whole.

With that as an introductory caveat, know that the text called Sigurd's Lament is a construction of three parts, a cacophony in three movements. First, there is the poem itself, which tells the tale of Alfred, Egil, and Sigurd—men of the ancient and fabled north, situated in the legendary lands of Elaea. Second, there are the footnotes that tell the tale of my family's engagement with a text that almost certainly instigated its downfall. Third, there is the introductory material, which tells the tale of the academic lineage of Sigurd's Lament, springing forth from my father's ingenuity.

Though I say that Sigurd's Lament should be swallowed whole, know that it is not—whole. It is fractured, fragmented, and distended. It is in itself meaningless. It is the swarming chaos of pandemonium in need of an authoritative reader that will mercilessly and forcefully both order and shape it into something worthwhile—into a thing that means. Is that you? Can it be? Perhaps it is everyone. All of us who seek to crack open a book and find within an infinity of distention. But perhaps it is no one. And Sigurd's Lament is nothing more than dead paper and lifeless words wrenched from a fictional reality.

I leave it to you.

Finding

When I was a boy living in London, my father told me stories of my Welsh grandfather, Basil Augustus Peters. According to my father, Wallace, Basil was only nineteen when it happened. It was 1867 and Basil was a sheep farmer in Aberdylwyth, a small coastal town south of Snowdonia Forest. Wallace referred to it as *Eryri*, but I was never good with the old language—a fact that my father reminded me of often.

Basil, he always started, was off tending sheep in the summer, near the hill of *Yr Wyddfa* or Snowdon. His prized sheep, Tylwyth, escaped him and so Basil, like any good shepherd, went deeper into the mountain in search of her. Before long, the day turned to night and Basil decided it would be better to camp near the summit and continue his search in the morning. He lit a small fire, sipped a bit of scotch, and sang himself to sleep. In the middling hours, however, when the moon was at its height, Basil was awakened by the sound of wood being thrown on the fire. To his surprise, he found a man—hoary headed and gray—sitting on a log next to his blanket. "Hail," the man said, "and well met."

"Who are you?"

"Me? Who are you?" The man's voice was deep and coarse.

"I'm Basil."

"Ah. I see. And me? I'm Rhitta. Rhitta Gawr. But some call me, Rhudda."

My grandfather sprang up and put the fire between he and Rhudda. "But you're a giant?"

"Well, perhaps, but I look ordinary enough, don't I?"

"Aye, you do. But all the same. I'll be asking you to leave now."

Rhudda laughed, a thick and hardy thing. "This is my mountain. I can't leave, even if I wanted to."

"Then give me my Tylwyth and I'll be on my way."

"I haven't got her," the giant shrugged.

"But—"

"I'll tell you what, I know your Tylwyth. I know where she is. She, unwittingly mind you, stumbled upon a . . . thing of worth. I can't have you bumbling about the mountainside and accidentally finding . . . well, *all* that Tylwyth has found. But I can lead her to you, in a safe manner. How does that sound?"

My grandfather grabbed his staff. "Let's go then."

"Ha!" Rhitta chortled. "I said, 'I'll bring her to you.' It's not—for it cannot be—the reverse. No sit, sit. There you go. Yes, that's right, that's right. Get comfortable. Ready? Here's what we'll do. If you can best me in a game of wits, then I'll let you live *and* return you to your little life."

My father stood. "You mean to kill me?"

"Sit down, sit down," Rhudda Gwar said while wringing his craggy hands. "You seem a smart lad, and I imagine you'll do just fine. But listen to the whole first before you make up your mind."

Basil nodded.

"Right then. If you can best me in a second game of wits, then I'll produce your Tylwyth. And if you can best me in a third game of wits, then I'll even give you one of the things—ancient and old—that Tylwyth has found. Now, being entirely up to you, Basil Augustus Peters, you can take your staff and leave my mountain with nothing worse for wear and tear. But you won't have your sheep, and there's simply nothing I can do about it. If, on the other hand, you desire to test your fate, then you can enter into a game of wits with I to gain your sheep or lose your life. At any point—one, two, or three—you can quit, but should you fail any *one* then stay you shall." The not-so-giant giant leaned forward. "Agreed?"

Basil looked to the fire and then Rhitta. "Agreed."

The Gwar clapped his hands in joy. "Then tell me Basil: What is dearer than light but deeper than sky, always skims the surface, but never ever lies?"

Sweat trickled down the back of Basil's hand as the hair on his head began to rise. Deep in the bowels of his innards, he thought: *I haven't a clue. I'll die here.* And then, like lightning from on high, he was struck by the answer. "Candor," he said, "it's candor!"

The giant laughed. "Well, you'll live. So I guess that's good. Shall we continue or would you like to escape the clutches of this old and evil man?"

"One more," Basil said. "I need Tylwyth. She's my family's fortune."

Rhudda grunted before continuing in the old language: "*Beth sy'n syrthio ond byth yn gostwng?*"

Basil stood. "I know this! Autumn. That's the answer —Autumn."

Rhitta began to tug his wiry beard. "Yes, I suppose that's true." He then snapped his fingers and, to Basil's astonishment, Tylwyth materialized next to Rhudda Gwar. "Here's your sheep," the giant said. "Now will you be on your way or will you play one more wit? Remember the price of failing, Basil."

The fire licked the remaining wood between Rhitta and Basil, casting odd shadows against the giant's face. Deep and ragged pockmarks lightly shown behind Rhudda's rough beard.

Tylwyth bleated.

"I'll play," Basil said. "Once more. I'll play."

Rhitta Gwar leaned forward. "How will I die?"

This is, of course, where my father would typically quit the story or, if he did not, then where my mother would interrupt. After all, death is not really a subject to be discussed with a six-year-old boy. But, as I grew older, I was able to piece together the rest of this fictional tale. I will recount it for you now, not because it is the truth behind the document's finding, but because it was that which my father *wanted* me to believe was the truth. For, as he would often say, "The line between reality and fiction is thin. And more often than not, it's the fiction that imbues our lives with meaning."[1]

Basil accepted the offer, for the pull of such a great and ancient thing was too strong to refuse. He could not, however, answer Rhitta Gwar's question: "How will I die?" According to my father's notes, he tried, but failed. Rhudda laughed and, rather than smite him on the spot, handed my father an archaic scroll and said, "What's written here will change your life for the better, but it's a twofold curse that will haunt you, your son, and your grandson." The curse was, or so my father claimed, the death of us all. It functioned in two ways: one, the individual in question would be captivated by the scroll's text, but would never be able to finish his life's work in relation to the text. My father died before he could complete both his translation and the academic apparatus surrounding his translation. He loved *Sigurd's Lament*, but it was the death of him. Two, the text would cause an irreparable rift between father and son for three generations. Basil refused to share his life with my great-great grandfather and died without having talked to him for forty-seven years. My father, Wallace, had a great falling out with Basil and knew of his death only through a newspaper obituary. And then there was me.

This is, of course, a great and noble fiction that my father internalized so as to excuse his behavior towards my mother and me. I reject it in favor of the historical truth. After my father died and I began to piece together his life's work, I found notes and scribbles recounting what really happened that night on Snowdon Mountain. This is what my father jotted down on one such note in a stack of papers marked, "Finding":[2]

> *Basil lost sheep. Went to find him. Common practice to throw stones into caves to see if sheep bleats. Too risky to enter by oneself. Basil stumbled upon cave. Threw rock. Heard something break. Entered cave. Found manuscript that we now know—Sigurd's Lament. Preserved all these years. Amazing. Claims the only text found. I wonder?*

1. Peters, *Notes and Letters*, 78.
2. Ibid., 87.

I cannot speak to multiple manuscripts, but I believe that this is the more accurate of the two stories. My grandfather went in search of a lost sheep, stumbled across a cave, and found within an old and ancient manuscript. While the former story is pure fancy, this latter is purely historical. While my father might be accustomed to making wild claims about fiction and truth, I more firmly root my epistemology in the concrete, the measurable, and the real.

Language

It has been said that "metrical practice is determined by the deeper music of language."[1] The manuscript I now have, however, is written in Medieval Welsh. And while it springs from the tradition of the Welsh poet Taliesin, it must be dated to the alliterative, Middle English revival sometime between 1350 and 1500.[2] The effect is rather alarming and works against the good sense of language's deeper music. While the poet wrote in an older form of Welsh, he almost certainly mimicked the poets of the revival.[3] The outcome is rather paradoxical: while thoroughly Welsh, *Sigurd's Lament* has nothing Welsh about it.

The Welsh Poets of the Nobility or the Cywyddwyr (CE 1300–1600) often wrote in a meter known as *cywydd*, which consists of a series of seven-syllable lines in rhyming couplets and all written in *cynghanedd*. I could commend no greater work to you on the subject than Meic Stephen's wonderful monograph.[4] But as I have said, the Sigurd Poet broke rank with his Welsh brethren and compiled something that, while utterly Welsh, is fully English. He wrote in Welsh, yes, but he wrote in what is known as the Middle English alliterative meter, which is a form of accentual poetry that neither counts syllables, as in syllabic poetry, nor a syllable's

---

1. Simpson, "Note on the Meter of the Alliterative *Morte Arthure*," 17.

2. Cf. Taliesin, *Taliesin Poems*.

3. Cf. Chism, *Alliterative Revivals*; Benson, "Date of the Alliterative Morte Arthure," 19–40; Tolkien, *Sir Gawain and the Green Knight*; Armitage, *Death of Arthur*; and Langland, *Piers Plowman*.

4. Stephens, *Oxford Companion to the Literature of Wales*.

length, as in quantitative poetry. The meter in *Sigurd's Lament* is both accented and alliterated. The latter being the "repetition of an initial consonant sound . . . in consecutive or closely positioned words."[5] It is important to remember that alliteration refers not to *letters*, but to *sounds*.[6]

Being the Middle English variety, *Sigurd's Lament* differs from its classical Anglo-Saxon brother, but it is—for the most part—standardized. When the poet sticks to the standard, the

> metrical pattern consists of two half lines, each with two accented syllables. These two half lines each form a syntactic unit, and are therefore separated by a caesura, or break, allowing a very small break in the recitation of such verse. The standard metrical pattern is *xx/xy*, where *x* signifies a stressed, alliterating syllable; / signifies a caesura; and *y* signifies a stressed, non-alliterating syllable. The second half line is thus linked to the first by the initial alliterating, stressed syllable.[7]

In its standardized form, the Middle English alliterative meter scans thusly: "The Green Knight on the ground / now gets himself ready."[8] Here it is easy to see that "Green," "ground," and "gets" are all accented syllables that alliterate. They are the *x* in the pattern. The final accented syllable, "ready," is the *y* in the pattern and does not alliterate. The /, of course, represents the caesura or the break in the line, which creates our two half lines with two accented syllables each. If this line were being read aloud, then the / would symbolize a short, breathless pause for the performer.

Alliteration, however, is a fluid form and as such is often played with throughout an alliterative poem. While there is a standardized form, it is often transgressed. One such example is taken from the *Alliterative Morte Arthure*: "for these folk are foreigners in the far-flung fields."[9] Here we see that the poet alliterated the

5. Armitage, *Death of Arthur*, 16.

6. Tolkien, *Legend of Sigurd and Gudrún*, 50.

7. Ibid., 16–17.

8. Tolkien, *Sir Gawain*, 29.

9. Armitage, *Death of Arthur*, 177.

final stressed syllable, breaking with the standardized format to create an *xx/xx* structure. This is but one example where, as we shall see, the Sigurd Poet takes many liberties and creates all manner of wild structuring: *yx/xx*, *xy/xx*, and *xx/yx*. It is important to remember throughout, however, that there is a standardized format and that it provides both the framework and *ideal* for the Sigurd Poet's metrical pattern.[10]

Any translator, of course, must decide how she will represent the meter not only in a new language foreign to the original language's deeper music, but also how she will reveal the meter's internal structure on the page. With alliterative meter, a translator has one of two options:

1 Then a powerful demon, a prowler through the dark,
    nursed a hard grievance. It harrowed him
    to hear the din of the loud banquet
    everyday in the hall, the harp being struck
    and the clear song of a skilled poet
    telling with mastery of man's beginnings.[11]

2 The Gods gathered
    on golden thrones,
    of doom and death
    deeply pondered,
    how fate should be fended,
    their foes vanquished,
    their labor healed,
    light rekindled.[12]

The first example, as can be seen, chooses to keep the caesura hidden resulting in each line being a full line of alliterative meter. The second, however, chooses to break the line at the caesura so that the reader can more easily encounter the poem's metrical structure. My father chose the latter, as will be seen, when

10. Cf. Bredehoft, *Early English Metre*; Cable, *English Alliterative Tradition*; Fulk, *History of Old English Meter*; Godden, "Literary Language," 490–535; Russom, *Beowulf and Old Germanic Metre*; and Goering, "*Fall of Arthur* and *The Legend of Sigurd and Gudrún*," 4–53.

11. Heaney, *Beowulf*, 5.

12. Tolkien, *Sigurd and Gudrún*, 61.

translating *Sigurd's Lament* Books I–V and VII–XI. He chose this, no doubt, to offset the variant metrical structures of Books VI and XII.

> 1 Sorrow and sadness
> saturate Elaea,
> for the king cannot
> come dawn arise.
> Winter wields
> its weary snow,
> burgeoning hopes
> bleakly low-brought.[13]

The *Sir Gawain and the Green Knight* poet, though alliterative, chose something altogether different. He employed what is commonly referred to as the "bob and wheel," where the "bob" is a very short line, sometimes of only two syllables, followed by the "wheel," longer lines with internal rhyme.[14] While the Gawain Poet utilized the bob and wheel throughout his poem, the Sigurd Poet only employed the bob and wheel in Books VI and XII. Three examples should suffice:

From J. R. R. Tolkien's archaic translation:

> 1 and far over the French flood Felix Brutus
> on many a broad bank and brae Britain established
> full fair,
> where strange things, strife and sadness,
> at whiles in the land did fare,
> and each other grief and gladness
> oft fast have followed there.[15]

The same passage from Simon Armitage's modern translation:

> 2 And further afield, over the Sea of France,
> on Britain's broad hilltops, Felix Brutus made
> his stand.
> And wonder, dread and war

13. *Sigurd's Lament*, II:1.

14. Brogan, "Bob and Wheel," 143.

15. Tolkien, *Sir Gawain*, 23–24.

have lingered in that land
where loss and love in turn
have held the upper hand.[16]

The Sigurd Poet's use of the bob and wheel:

3 "From emptiness then, forged and fashioned,
the Makers created matter and spirit
and form."
Enigmatic Edward
pauses and prepares
his wondrous word-hoard
to dispense crucial cares.[17]

While the poet's choice to utilize the bob and wheel in Books VI and XII is lost to history, my father believed that it was to offset the nature of the content.[18] In Book VI, the poet is dealing with Elaea's creation mythology, and in Book XII he is working through the eponymous matter of Sigurd's lamentation. Whatever the reason, the shift from the ideal form of alliterative meter to the bob and wheel is effective in cluing the reader into special content, in breaking the monotony of the standardized form, and in exposing the poet's versatility.

To answer the question posed so long ago: why is the poet both Welsh and English? The poet not only writes in old Welsh, but also invokes the Welsh bards and skalds, lore and geography, and ethos and spirit, especially as represented by the Northerners, Egil and Sigurd. The poet, however, is equally interested in taking this picture of Welsh-ness or North-ness and synthesizing it with all that is English, its meter and language, cosmology and custom, and tradition and heritage, especially as represented by the Southerners, Alfred and Edward. What we have then is not so much a culturally monolithic epic, but rather a poem plagued by the poet's own complex culture, bibliography, and imagination.

16. Armitage, *Sir Gawain*, 21.

17. *Sigurd's Lament*, VI:1.

18. Peters, *Notes and Letter*, 781.

What we find in *Sigurd's Lament* is a cacophony of influence, style, texture, and culture. It is Welsh in language, but English in structure. It is standardized alliteration, but varies greatly in its use of the bob and wheel. While Taliesin and the Middle English poets influence it, so too does the epic poetry of Greece, Italy, and England. And while my father's translation reads well in English—it is, in fact, magnificent—it cannot approach the tone and timbre of the original language's deeper music.

The complexity of the Sigurd Poet's linguistic and metrical choices all point towards one end: the fictive. For where else can all roads lead to one, coalescing in nothing less than the process of creation itself?

Translation

My father was born Welsh, but grew up English. At home he spoke Welsh with both my grandfather and mother, but at work he spoke English. He was a cultural bastard with no place to call home. "I speak in English," he often said, "but I think in Welsh."[1] Though this fact uniquely positioned him to translate a text like *Sigurd's Lament*, it is important to remember that taking the poetry of one language and forcing it into the rigidity of a foreign language is no easy task. We often take the entire process for granted, especially with our sacred texts. But let me be paradoxically clear: *Sigurd's Lament* was not written in English and you lose something by not reading it in the original. My father knew it. I know it. And you should, too. If you cannot read old Welsh—and the original manuscript is both on display at the Royal Museum and available online—then my father's translation is more than sufficient.

I say paradoxically clear, however, because while my father's translation is not the same as the "original" Welsh version, I readily believe the idea or concept of the original does not exist. This, of course, raises the typical questions of translation.[2] What is a poem to its language? Where does it exist? In the original alone? Or does the aesthetic transcend language, making its home in some

---

1. Peters, *Notes and Letters*, 1032.

2. Cf. Schulte and Biguenet, *Theories of Translation*; Biguenet and Schulte, *Craft of Translation*; Raffel, *Art of Translating Prose*; Raffel, *Art of Translating Poetry*.

neo-Platonic nether? If I have only read Homer's *Odyssey* in English, then can it be said that I have read it at all?

Here is what I am getting at: the poem in English is not the poem in Welsh and the poem in Welsh is not the poem in English, and neither one makes an authoritative claim. This niggling fact might make you uncomfortable—and it should!—but what other truth do we have? My father's translation is not the original, but it is most certainly not secondary to the original. In other words, it exists in a literary spacetime as its own authentic work. And let that be enough.

Author

Who is the author of *Sigurd's Lament*? We simply do not know. Any theoretical claim to state otherwise is simply wrong. For a full discussion on the authorship of *Sigurd's Lament*, I would ask that you consult those scholars that find it rather stimulating to ruminate on the unsolvable mysteries of textual histories. I would particularly point you towards: James L. Wintrow and Alistair M. Hobson.[1] And the best of luck to you.

The only thing that *I* will state on the matter is that the tight alliteration of the first three books have led many to assume that *Sigurd's Lament* is a compilation of two or more writers. Though many, there are only two hypotheses worth mentioning. The first is put forth by Wintrow and widely accepted. His theory is that Books I–III were written by an early Briton sometime in the first half of the twelfth century and that Books IV–XII were completed sometime later by the "Revival Poet" throughout the Alliterative Revival.

Hobson posits the second theory. It is his minority position that the poem was written at the tail end of the Alliterative Revival by a coterie of poets living in community. "The fractured and disjointed alliteration, the word choice and cadence, and the roving narrative," Hobson suggests, "all point to a collection of writers rather than *a* writer."[2] I will leave it to the reader to make his or her decision, but—full disclosure—do know that my father sided

1. Cf. *Sigurd's Lament* I:1 n. 151; Wintrow, *Cat and Chalice*, 8–23; and Hobson, *Through the Windows of Poetry*, 37–48.

2. Hobson, *Through the Windows of Poetry*, 37–48.

with Wintrow in this most heated of academic debates, which I find rather frivolous.

Let us now leave well enough alone and move on to that which, with relative confidence, we can say.

Historicity and Genre

There are those that claim a text is only valuable insofar as it is historically verifiable, whatever that might mean.[1] Truth and fact—the latter a post-Enlightenment construction—are not the same entities. A text can be empirically false *and* wholly true. "To write is to create," my father always said, "and to create is to lie. This is what we've been given, the greatest gift of all: the power of untruth."[2]

A complex statement to untangle, yes, but compelling nonetheless.

So what does it *mean* that Elaea is divorced from our concept of mapping or geography?[3] Does the historical inaccuracy of *Sigurd's Lament* undo the poem? Is the creative work any different, really, from the historical work?[4]

By way of exploring these questions, my father—in his *Notes and Letters*—placed *Sigurd's Lament* within its larger, epic context. To call something "epic" is to make a claim about its style, structure, and, to a degree, content. Building on William Harmon's epic conventions,[5] my father went to great lengths to show the how and the why of *Sigurd's Lament's* inclusion in that category. While there

---

1. Cf. Blomberg, *Historical Reliability of the Gospels*, and Bird, *How God Became Jesus,* on the one hand, and Borg, *Jesus*, and Ehrman, *How Jesus Became God*, on the other.

2. W. W. Peters, *Notes and Letters*, 3.

3. "Meaning" is itself a problematic and ambiguous term.

4. Cf. Cavendish, "Blazing World."

5. Cf. Harmon, *Handbook to Literature.*

are numerous conventions or characteristics of an epic, I will only highlight four before commending Harmon's work to the reader. It is there that one can continue to explore the many ways in which *Sigurd's Lament* fits well within the tradition of the epic poem.

1. It begins *in medias res*:

> Scribe doth score,
> set in runes,
> the song now sung—
> Sigurd's Lament.
> Drama in mezzo,
> midway begun:
> "Harken! from Sherwood,
> hither a rider breaks."[6]

2. It includes the heroic present, epithets, and formal speeches, as well as heroes that embody the values of their civilization—in this case, the nations of Elaea: Elaea and Umbria. I would particularly point you towards Books V–VI for numerous examples of these four features.

3. It includes vast settings, covering many nations, divine interventions on human affairs, and the tragic hero's descent into the underworld. See Books III–V and X–XII.

4. It includes an epic invocation:

> Sing, O Bard,
> sit and tell,
> of benevolent hero
> bidding life,
> ascending to Avalonia,
> arising in grief,
> despairing death
> of dear kindred.
>
> Sing, O Bard,
> sit and tell,
> of Sigurd's actions,
> afterwards wrought:
> of marching on Caerpel,

6. *Sigurd's Lament*, I:4.

of marauders besetting,
of loved ones low-brought,
of lurid transgressions.

Scribe doth score,
set in runes,
the song now sung—
Sigurd's Lament.
Drama in mezzo,
midway begun.[7]

The epic invocation particularly interested my father. In one of his many posthumous piles that I unearthed laying about his study, I found one filled with nothing but invocations pulled from various epics. I will highlight a few of these, as my father believed it to be important to the overall context of *Sigurd's Lament*. In other words, he wanted his poem digested alongside what he almost certainly viewed as the greater ones.

1. Rage—Goddess, sing the rage of Peleus' son Achilles, / Murderous, doomed, that cost the Achaeans countless losses, / hurling down to the House of Death so many sturdy souls, / great fighters' souls, but made their bodies carrion, / feasts for the dogs and birds, / and the will of Zeus was moving towards its end. / Begin, Muse, when the two first broke and clashed, / Agamemnon lord of men and brilliant Achilles.[8]

2. Sing to me of the man, Muse, the man of twists and turns / driven time and again off course, once he had plundered / the hallowed heights of Troy . . . Launch out on his story, Muse, daughter of Zeus, / start from where you will—sing for our time too.[9]

3. Mother of Aeneas and of his Rome, and of gods / and men the joy, dear Venus, who underneath the gliding / heavenly signals busies the seas with ships and makes / earth fruitful (for only through you are living things

7. Ibid., I:1.
8. Homer, *Iliad*, 77.
9. Homer, *Odyssey*, 77.

conceived / and because of you they rise up to bask in the light of the sun) / . . . except by you, and nothing joyful or lovely is made. / I seek, therefore, your blessing and help in writing these verses / that I presume to compose on the Nature of Things, the way / things come about and are.[10]

4. Of bodies changed to other forms I tell; / You Gods, who have yourselves wrought every change, / Inspire my enterprise and lead my lay / In one continuous song from nature's first / Remote beginnings to our modern times.[11]

5. Wars and a man I sing—an exile driven on by Fate, / he was the first to flee the coast of Troy, / destined to reach Lavinian shores and Italian soil, / yet many blows he took on land and sea from the gods above— / thanks to cruel Juno's relentless rage . . . Tell me the causes now, O Muse, how galled / In her divine pride, and how sore at heart / From her old wound, the queen of gods compelled him— / A man apart, devoted to his mission— / To undergo so many perilous days . . . / Can anger / Black as this prey on the minds of heaven?[12]

6. Wars worse than civil we sing, waged on Emathia's plains; / Justice given over to crime; . . . / Still, if the Fates have found no other way for Nero's advent, / if an everlasting dynasty costs the Gods dear, / then, O Gods Above, we make no further complaint: / even such crimes and evil are not too high a price for this purchase / let Pharsalia soak its dreadful plains, / and let the Punic ghost be glutted with blood; / Rome is nonetheless much indebted to civil arms, / since all was done for you! / But to me, you are already divine: if I, a seer, / have you in my heart, . . . / you are enough to make Roman poetry vital! / . . . Great things fall in on themselves: this limit Divinity sets / on the growth of prosperous states.[13]

10. Lucretius, *De Rerum Natura*, 1–2.

11. Ovid, *Metamorphoses*, 1.

12. Virgil, *Aeneid*, I:1–19.

13. Lucan, *Pharsalia*, 1–6.

7. We have heard tell / of the high doings / of Danish kings / in days gone by, / how the great war-chiefs / gained their renown, how Scyld Scefing / shattered his foes, / mastered the meadhalls / of many peoples, / conquered their kings.[14]

8. In the middle of the journey of our life / I came to myself in a dark wood / where the straight way was lost . . . / O Muses, O high Genius, now help me! / O Memory, that hast inscribed what I saw, / here will be shown thy nobleness.[15]

9. May great, glorious God, through His singular grace, / And the precious prayers of His peerless Mother, / Help us shun shameful ways and wicked works, / And grant us grace to guide and govern us here, / In this woeful world, through virtuous ways, / That we may hurry to His court, / the Kingdom of Heaven, / . . . And help me to pour forth some words here and new, / neither empty nor idle, only honor to him, / And pleasing and helpful to all people who hear.[16]

10. I sing of war, of holy war, and him, / Captain who freed the Sepulchre of Christ . . . / O Muse, not you who upon Helicon . . . / but you who among heavenly choir don / your golden crown of deathless stars always: / breathe in my breast celestial fire, shed on / my song your light, and pardon if my lays, / embroidering the truth, seem overgrown / at time with pleasures other than your own.[17]

11. Sing heavenly Muse, that on the secret top / Of Oreb, or of Sinai, didst inspire / That shepherd, who first taught the chosen seed . . . / I thence / Invoke thy aid to my advent'rous song, / That with no middle flight intends to soar / Above the Aonian mount.[18]

---

14. Ringler, *Beowulf*, 3.

15. Dante, *Divine Comedy*, 11 and 17.

16. Krishna, *Alliterative "Morte Arthure,"* 1.

17. Tasso, *Liberation of Jerusalem*, 3.

18. Milton, *Paradise Lost*, 59.

12. May all love, / His love, unseen but felt, o'ershadow Thee, / The love of all Thy sons encompass Thee, / The love of all Thy daughters cherish Thee, / The love of all Thy people comfort Thee, / Till God's love see Thee at his side again![19]

13. Lady, by one light only / We look from Alfred's eyes, / We know he saw athwart the wreck / The sign that hangs about your neck, / Where One more than Melchizedek / Is dead and never dies. / Therefore I bring these rhymes to you / Who brought the cross to me, / Since on you flaming without flaw / I saw the sign that Guthrum saw / When he let break his ship of awe, / And laid peace on the sea.[20]

14. Attention I ask from all the sacred people, / greater and lesser, the offspring of Heimdall; / Father of the Slain, / you wished that I should declare / the ancient histories of men and gods, those which I / remember from the first . . . / I know that an ash-tree stands called Yggdrasill, / a high tree, soaked with shining loam; / from there come the dews which fall in the valley, / ever green, it stands over the well of fate.[21]

15. Of old was an age / when was emptiness, / there was sand nor sea / nor surging waves . . . / The Great Gods then / began their toil . . . / A seer long silent / her song upraised . . . / Of doom and death / dark words she spake, / of the last battle / of the leaguered Gods.[22]

---

19. Tennyson, *Idylls of the King*, 20. Though not strictly an invocation, my father included it for two reasons: one, its influence on the poet cannot be overstated and, two, by invoking the name of Albert and the importance of the Queen in the life of the English, Tennyson is, in a way, calling upon his Muse.

20. Chesterton, *Ballad of the White Horse*, ix.

21. Larrington, *Poetic Edda*, 6. Here we have not an invocation to the Muses, but rather to the people, the people of the gods. My father included it here, no doubt, because he thought it beautiful.

22. Tolkien, *Sigurd and Gudrún*, 61 and 64. Though not strictly an invocation, my father included Tolkien out of both a sense of duty and belief that he strongly influenced the Sigurd Poet in a Bayardian instance of anticipatory plagiarism.

16. Thus the tides of time / to turn backward / and the heathen to humble, / his hope urged him, / that with harrying ships / they should hunt no more / on the shining shores . . . / As when the earth dwindles / in autumn days / and soon to its setting / the sun is waning / under mournful mist, / then a man will lust / for work and wandering, / while yet warm floweth / blood sun-kindled, / so burned his soul / after long glory / for a last assay / or pride and prowess, / to the proof setting / will unyielding / in war with fate.[23]

At the end of his invocation list, on a crumpled and yellowing paper, my father penned: "There lies the port." I can only assume that this is in reference to Alfred Lord Tennyson's *Ulysses*, but why, I cannot say. Beneath this, he wrote:

> *Plato kicked the poets out—yes. Aristotle reinstalled them: "Imitation is the instinct of our nature."[24] But for me, Boccaccio and Tasso. From the former: "Poetry from God is always rare in humanity,"[25] and from the latter: "I say that the heroic poem is an imitation of an action noble, great, and perfect, narrated in the loftiest verse, with the aim of giving profit through delight."[26] I wonder. Always. Is this still possible?[27]*

I can only speculate as to my father's frame of mind when he wrote this, but perhaps my father compiled this list to reassure himself during one of his episodes of intense doubt, which he often had.

23. Tolkien, *Lord of the Rings*, 17. Though not strictly an invocation, my father firmly believed that Tolkien belonged on every literary list ever made, hence his second inclusion here.

24. Adams and Searle, *Critical Theory since Plato*, 31–38 and 52.

25. Ibid., 160.

26. Ibid., 231.

27. W. W. Peters, *Notes and Letters*, 56.

Major Concerns

I will now engage what I consider to be the major concerns of *Sigurd's Lament*. This includes, but is not limited to: major themes; religion, myth, and poetry; the nature of narrative; my father's academic work in both distended reception and hermeneutical clusters; and finally, the reception both critical and otherwise of *Sigurd's Lament*. I will forgo any lengthy introduction and ask only that you read with rapt attention.

MAJOR THEMES

In this section, I will explore the major themes of *Sigurd's Lament* as I see them. Not everyone agrees with me, however. For a thorough analysis of the most recent criticism on *Sigurd's Lament*, see Andrew Jorgenson's well-wrought tome.[1]

Fate

The role of fate in *Sigurd's Lament* cannot be overstressed. While modern readers with their eyes accustomed to the psychological choices with which characters wrestle will no doubt find this distasteful, I only ask that any reader recall the distant past from whence *Sigurd's Lament* comes into view. This poem is from a different age with unknown literary goals. Its sights are set on alien shores. Who are we—we who think only of ourselves—to judge a

---

1. Cf. Jorgenson, *Of Gods and Men*.

work that asks something more from us? I ask with the poet: "Frail may we be, / but damn the gods / for damning us so. / For who are they / to throw their stones?"[2]

Legacy

Throughout the poem, we see the concept of legacy weighing heavily on its principal characters. Alfred is concerned with Elaea's; Edward is attentive to Alfred's; Egil cares only for Umbria's; and Sigurd's mind is set on Sigurd's. The decisions that each character must make throughout the poem are in direct relation to a legacy contrasting a fate. Will he or wont he leave a legacy promulgated by an "action noble, great, and perfect?"[3] In other words, one concern for the Sigurd Poet is that age-old conflict between legacy and fate.

In *Sigurd's Lament*, the poet is carving out a space to creatively discuss the ways in which fate is not a pre-written script, but rather that thing crafted by the accumulated actions of both humans and gods alike. It might appear as if fate is preordained when Jupiter questions the stars: "Who am I— / wonderful to behold— / to raze fate or / ruin time? / 'Jupiter,' you say, / 'the joyous god,' / but what's a name / that wants in power? / Even I, a deity, / must e'er deign to stars."[4] But it must be remembered, Jupiter's perspective is that of the culture's from whence the poet derives. At every turn, he is pushing against the cultural norm, asking the readers of *Sigurd's Lament* to reject any notion of historical teleology. In the end, the poet says, we make or kill history, but the choice is ours. "May you," the poet writes, "mine hearts and hearers / who bear history's burdens, / triumph o'er tyrannical error / and evil ever determined."[5]

---

2. *Sigurd's Lament*, X:34.

3. This is, of course, Tasso. Cf. Adams and Searle, *Critical Theory since Plato*, 231.

4. *Sigurd's Lament*, VII:6–7.

5. Ibid., XII:34.

Validity of War

War, according the Sigurd Poet, is folly. Though much of the plot centers on the *holmgang* conducted between Alfred and Egil, the poet in no way glorifies battle. This is best seen through Sigurd's actual lament in Book XII:

> "My soul quakes," young Sigurd speaks, / "when I went to war I rode in anger. / I bumbled through battle as a bringer of death. / I hacked and hewed and Hel I wrought . . . / Such sickness is sought in the slicing melee, / a wrath revealed in the wonderment of / cosmos. / Philosophers play / at unknotting knowledge, / but by that betray / our constructed collage."[6]

The poet claims that violence, though sickening, is a reflection of what humanity sees in nature. Yet, at the end of the stanza, we see the poet professing that both our knowledge and perspectives on it are nothing more than constructions. In other words, what does the sun or the moon or the cosmos know of violence? Nothing. To name a thing "violent" and then to claim that it is a reflection of nature is to betray an anthropocentric epistemology, which the poet finds rather distasteful. Anthropocentric or not, however, the poet believes violence to be equally distasteful.

In Book III, we read of Alfred's clash with Anglach. What should be a moment of idealized violence becomes "folly unmasked" in which "the king lay dying."[7] And yet, laying silently beneath the text is an undertone of admiration. "I'll not strike," the poet writes, "Ill treated!"[8] If violence is abhorrent, then at least Alfred's condescension to it is laudable.

I must here, however, betray my own beliefs. I think war is evil, a blot on human existence. Does my personal conviction color the way in which I read *Sigurd's Lament*?[9] Perhaps. I cannot say. But if mine changes the text, then so too yours. My father

6. Ibid., XII:2.
7. Ibid., III:23, 31.
8. Ibid., III:28.
9. Yuri, "Peters' Folly in All Things," 32–90.

thought well of the Sigurd Poet, but believed him overly interested in matters of savagery.[10] This, no doubt, had to do with my father's own time on the continent, fighting in trenches throughout WWI. But why should his *experience* jeopardize his *interpretation*?

In the end, the Sigurd Poet has his own ideas about violence, war, and anthropocentric epistemologies. To read the poem is to enter into a complex world of significations, meanings, and interpretations that once characterized a human being's enfleshed experience. To reduce that to one, singular and monolithic, interpretation is a grave error. Reader, be warned. I will, however, leave you with these fitting words from the poet himself:

> Be neither keen nor quick
> to stand in court
>
> and preemptively pronounce
> a pitiable judgment
> upon the proud warrior
> who precedes to war.
> We, we in comfort,
> are without the burdens
> brought on by slaughter
> that surface from blood.
>
> We who will labor
> and work for bread,
> know not the knight
> who kills in kind.
> Weep we may
> for woeful warrior,
> but to question and query
> is cancerous indeed.[11]

10. Peters, *Notes and Letters*, 88–92.
11. *Sigurd's Lament*, XI:4–6.

Language as Meaningless

"Neither time nor language," the poet writes, "exists in stasis."[12] He continues, recounting the creation of Elaea:

> Words thus spoken, were vital to Jüt
> who witnessed the speaking wielded by firsts.
> Language inaugurated, likewise so time,
> with plentiful words wondrous in sum.
> Bequeathed in echoes, however, is our bereft speech,
>> which desires
>> meaning meted by use
>> but pales poorly
>> when compared with words loosed
>> by august architects orally.
>
> So sign and referent were sown in synthesis,
> and happily Jüt honed his skill—
> whole-words worked to weave whole worlds.[13]

The poet is making wildly exaggerated claims. For him, language as it now exists betrays an arbitrary disjunction between a sign and its referent.[14] This is not new. What he suggests, however, is that there was a time—unfathomable to conceive—when sign and referent were one and, as such, capable of creating whole worlds. Jüt, who first wielded this word-power, instantiated spacetime as we know it, but so also set in motion the inevitable chasm between language and meaning. This theme continually plays throughout the poem. "Caught in the cacophony / of cruel history," the poet writes in Book XI, "Propelled forward / by privileged time, / . . . our doomed warriors / dismount and prepare / . . . Then before time / can thoroughly arrest, / the clashing and clanging / of cold steel rings forth."[15] Sign and referent are split, spacetime is created,

---

12. Ibid., VI:1.

13. Ibid., VI:2.

14. Cf. Saussure, *Course in General Linguistics.* The poet was, obviously, well aware of linguistics, analytic philosophy, and the role of language in creating the human experience.

15. *Sigurd's Lament*, XI:1–4.

and its expansion is likened to an unceasing beat. All of us, gods and kings, are trapped atop its hammered anvil.

Since humanity is forever separated from referent (language from meaning), it is evermore incapable of grasping *Being*. For the poet, this chasm cannot be crossed. What was divorced in the beginning can never be reconciled. If you like, then for the poet the constant mediation that language plays in experience is the result of the fall, the first sin. To analogize the poet's position to Christian categories, however, does little justice to the "pagan" outlook of the Sigurd Poet. His worldview was and is harsh, and in it there is little room for either redemption or reconciliation. If there is a hope that exists in Elaea, then it does not exists within a linguistic framework.

Is meaning then possible for the poet? Yes. It is found through the grid of hermeneutical clusters circumscribing an injected, if arbitrary, narrative.[16] Where these narratives originate and how they escape the cycle of linguistic despair is a mystery. What matters to the poet, however, is that adherents to a particular narrative are faithful to that narrative. "Mystery," he writes, "or rather, mysteries / proliferate plentifully, / when hammered by history / we fail to be faithful."[17] How does one remain faithful? By acting in an uncertain world: "From what far corner shall faith be kept? / . . . Alfred, / to precipitate proud victory / in that final fray, / must be loosed from heaven's history / and travel to death's day."[18] In other words, for faith to be kept with this necessary Elaean narrative, Alfred must choose to act, though acting will result in his certain death.

In a strange twist, language for the poet is meaningless, even though it was through language that his world was and is created. And while this causes the poet great despair, it also results in the eventual solution to his rather grim problem—poetic action. While this may not be satisfactory to some,[19] I find it rather elegant.

16. See below, "Why Is Narrative?," "Distention's Bloom," and "Hermeneutical Clusters."

17. Ibid., VI:14.

18. Ibid., VI:17.

19. Tatombo, *Exalted Reaches*, 311–56.

Perspective

In his boldest move, the poet creates an impression throughout Books I–IX that Elaea and Alfred are the right, true, and just, only to wipe it all away in Books X–XII. What is first signified as good, Alfred's eager pursuit of lawful justice against Egil, later turns into Egil's righteous and deserved undoing of Elaean oppression. "Would that we could wend / our way through fate," the poet writes, "and find our fabled lives, / but both tales and truth / have this in common: / they are constructed / from experience's cloth, / neither factual nor real— / never fully known."

The poet suggests that truth is dependent upon the position of the one considering it. This is a theme that he returns to again and again, but most noticeably in the structuring of the poem as a whole. Within the narrative itself, this is both first and best seen in Egil's speech to his men on the eve of that fated *holmgang*. "Long have we labored . . . / oppressed and persecuted / by a privileged few. / But why? I beg. / Do I not bleed . . . / Does my mind not mutate / when mastered overlong? / Does my war-weary wife / warrant less than Alfred's?"[20] Not only does the poet humanize Egil, but he also provides him with the moral high ground. "Yes," the reader wants to say, "yes. Why have you been oppressed by Alfred, the king I've been rooting for all along?"[21]

The poet does not answer. For the poet, there is no answer. This is life in all its complexity, and we best choose our heroes carefully. The poet is not done with problematizing perspective, however. The entirety of Book X is dedicated to this effort. I heartily commend it to the reader. There the poet jumps from one end of the battlefield to the other, allowing the reader to see the inner lives of both Magnus and Eustice on Egil's side *and* Crispin and Marius on Alfred's side. Each is right in their own way, but I would particularly point out Eustace's role in murdering Magnus and manipulating Sigurd. Is Eustace wrong in what he does? According to the poet, no. Eustace is not evil or wrong in his action, rather he

---

20. *Sigurd's Lament*, IX:9–11.

21. Darling, *Problem with Perspective*, 98–117.

is only a man yearning for more from life.[22] For him, Umbria will be free and there is no price too high to pay. Who among us can naysay the sly Northerner?

In the end, the poet finds perspective and position troubling. He is in no way glorifying the ambiguity of history, only acknowledging it as such and lamenting the inability of humanity to find a coherent and cohesive way forward. In fact, the poet finds history rather bleak. "Does thou thrive / 'pon thirsty blades," he writes, "or sheathing swords / for ending strife? / The choice is thine / but choose thee well, / for the grinding stones / of sorrowful history / once set in motion, / cannot unset be."[23] Sigurd, in all his victorious melancholy, answers the poet: "For this is truth, terrible and yawning: / all we mold and pretend to master / is the present matter, a primordial motion / crashing and clanging and canceling progress. We pretend and profess that history is pointed, / but victory is random and rarely righteous."[24] It is through Sigurd then that the poet posits the most deflating of historical questions: why should a coherent and cohesive teleology be preferable to humankind when historical experience reveals something far more oceanic, fluid, and indeterminate?

RELIGION, MYTH, OR POETRY?

My father scratched this question atop his penultimate translation of *Sigurd's Lament*. It always struck me as odd that he would choose these three categories to describe the poem, but for him, as I have come to find, religion, myth, and poetry[25] comprised the holy trinity of meaning creation. The only academic paper that he wrote—though it went unpublished until now—was on just this topic. But before I present you with his ideas on the necessary

---

22. *Sigurd's Lament*, X:7.

23. Ibid., XI:30–31.

24. Ibid., XII:3.

25. Science is a sad and lamentable omission from my father's list of meaning making.

condition of narrative, I will turn my attention to showing how each category is itself represented throughout the poem.

Gods and Heroes

If you are reading this, then you no doubt know that I cut my academic teeth on the study of religion. It is only natural then that my first book[26] on *Sigurd's Lament* was an exploration into the vast and various ways in which Elaea both thinks about and embodies its various religions.[27] I will not recount the whole of the book here. I will exercise great restraint, and only provide you with the roughest of sketches for better understanding one piece of the puzzle that is *Sigurd's Lament*.

The poet introduces the Elaean conception—at least the southern Elaean understanding—of religion early in his work. In Book I:13, Alfred comments, "Let us, O people, / a pyre construct / to burn mine cousin's / crimson cloak. / Gods will forgive, / great as they are, / for lacking in lamentation, / a lifeless body." The gods, however, do not forgive. While the poet does not tell us why Edward enters Hel instead of Avalonia, we can only assume that the poet is here subtly critiquing the gods. They are not, it would appear, as forgiving as Alfred would like them to be. This, however, is only the first piece of the religious puzzle that comprises *Sigurd's Lament*.

Crispin, after the king descends into his coma, calls together his generals. They decide that in an effort to raise their king from the depths of his unconscious, they will "call for priests / to conduct a service / in honor of Alfred, / the un-healed king."[28] The

---

26. Cf. H. B. Peters, *Religion in the Life of Sigurd*.

27. Cf. Geertz, *Interpretation of Cultures*, 90, and Orsi, *Between Heaven and Earth*, 5, for in-depth and astute analyses into the various ways in which religious scholars engage their object of study. Spoiler alert: Geertz is interested in the signs and symbols of religion while Orsi is interested in the ways in which religions are lived. Double spoiler alert: their positions are not that different, though Orsi would certainly like you to believe that they are.

28. *Sigurd's Lament*, II:6.

clerics come and officiate over an incense offering only to find their "pleas unanswered."[29] The poet, again, offers a sly critique of both Elaea's religion—we do not know if it is his own—and Elaea's embedded ecclesiastical hierarchy. Less than midway through Book II then, we find that the poet has already criticized the gods, their priests, and the cultural power structures that hold Elaea's religions together.

When Alfred eventually enters Avalonia, we find the poet describing it as a kind of neo-Platonic nether wherein a flawless justice forever reigns.[30] It is a place of which Alfred can say, "Life a wraith . . . / a shadow of truth, / 'till now unknown."[31] What at first appears to be a wholesale rejection of the gods and their religion is a much more complex and nuanced critique of the religion that he, the poet, currently finds throughout his world. For example, the Gate-Keeper leads Alfred to the edges of Hel, sharing with the king that all is not as it appears in Avalonia. The Gate-Keeper is filled with "tales e're-mournful."[32] It is as if the poet is calling his readers away from the view that the mutable should forever be contrasted with the immutable. Perhaps, he asks, it is the opposite? That which is changeless only has meaning in respect to that which changes.[33] The poet, in other words, is posing a question to his readers, an age-old question: Perhaps Lucretius was right?[34] And if not, then who cares? Life is short and grim, but beautiful and filled with some little joy, however difficulty attained.

And still, the poet is not finished with religion. In *Sigurd's Lament*, we see the reign of hate and violence in Hel,[35] the condescension and dissension of the gods in Avalonia,[36] and the humility and

---

29. Ibid., II:7.

30. Ibid., II:13.

31. Ibid., II:15.

32. Ibid., II:21.

33. Cf. Smolin, *Time Reborn*.

34. Lucretius, *De Rerum Natura*, and Xanthu, "Swerve and Spin," 901–1201.

35. *Sigurd's Lament*, III:8–12.

36. Ibid., III:22–31.

wisdom of Jupiter.[37] All of these revelations reflect a poet who is, though deeply ambivalent, compelled by religion, faith, and that which seeks to wrest meaning from the world. He seems to be what my father called "a reverent agnostic,"[38] a human being who lives and breathes and seeks, but is no more certain of reality than the ambiguity of the saints. "The gods are gracious," the poet writes, "when gain they see, / but clearly capricious / when conflicting wants / muddle their manifested / desires 'pon mortals."[39]

Where the world is grim and dark and filled with despair,[40] the heavens yearn for that which is mutable.[41] Where the gods present choices as if they were theirs to employ,[42] Jupiter betrays his own obligation to both fate and time.[43] Where the gods and their clerics boast truth and justice,[44] the poet sees only violence and hatred.[45] To account for these paradoxes, I would locate the voice of the poet firmly within Sigurd's speech: "Philosophers play / at unknotting knowledge, / but by that betray / our constructed collage."[46]

Though this, at first glance, might be disheartening to modern readers, neither the poem nor the poet is without hope. But for that, we must turn to the men and women, the primary actors in *Sigurd's Lament*, and affirm their places within the narrative.

Women and Men

While much criticism has been leveled against the portrayal or lack thereof of women in *Sigurd's Lament*, I believe these criticisms

37. Ibid., VII:5–8.
38. W. W. Peters, *Notes and Letters*, 412.
39. *Sigurd's Lament*, X:15.
40. Ibid., XI:34.
41. Ibid., II:20–21, 25–26.
42. Ibid., XI:30–31.
43. Ibid., VII:5–8.
44. Ibid., XII:6.
45. Ibid., XII:7.
46. Ibid., XII:2.

to be misguided.[47] I rest this claim squarely on the shoulders of Flora.[48] Where the ultimate god, the masculine Jüt, is bound by both fate and time, the feminine Flora—the goddess of spring, alchemy, crafting, and poetry—is one of the poem's rare agents. She is able to move through heaven and earth and act in such a way that no other character is able. She can see the future, but unlike Jüt is unafraid of what the Elaean Ragnarök will bring. She is able to make choices, act in the world, and bring her desires to fruition. This can be said of no other character. She also happens to be the principal signification of hope, if it can be called that, within the Elaean schema.[49] This is, of course, reflected in the importance of the crocus for both the poet and the nation of Elaea.

In the myth and lore of Elaea, the crocus flower—a small, blue thing—is the first bloom of spring. It heralds the fall of winter and the reign of the coming summer. Flora is, being the goddess of spring, often worshiped and praised upon the finding of the first crocus. It is her doing that both brings the flower and banishes winter.

In Book XI, when the kings meet in the thicket of Kore to treat and perchance find a way out of their predicament, a crocus is spotted. For the poet, this signifies that all is not lost—hope remains. "The Elaean crocus," he writes, "Winter's Bane, so called, / for its blue bloom / is winter's blue death."[50] And yet, men and warriors in their bloodlust often forget the goddess of spring, the one who acts in partnership with humankind. Notice that as the battle commences on the fated day of Alfred and Egil's death, it is not the killing and warfare that the poet laments, but the crushing of hope as seen in the trampling of the crocus once thriving between the two battling armies: "Rushing and writhing, / like

---

47. Warmhurst, *Sex in Sigurd*, 246; Wilby, *Voices of Sigurd*, 57; Vertincort, *Kore and the Love of Spring*, 316; Vandergaarde, *Killing in the Name Of*, 34–98; Sopkje, "Tides of Poetry in Community," 152–73; N. V. Peters, *Sexism in Alliterative Verse*, 172–84; and N. V. Peters, *Women at Play*, 202–67.

48. Mabeuf, *Flora of the Environs of Cauteretz*, 67.

49. Hunt, *Crocus for Your Thoughts*, 12.

50. *Sigurd's Lament*, IX:20.

a roiling torrent, / the armies clash / on the spring-crisp field. / Where crocuses bloomed, / now battle tramps— / men lost to lust / forgetting their lords."[51]

Why, in a section exploring the representations of men and women in the poem, discuss a goddess and the flower that signifies her? Because as I have argued elsewhere and my father argued throughout his life, Flora is the poet's ideal or archetype for men and women moving in the world.[52] There are no weak characters in *Sigurd's Lament*. There *are* characters plagued by their own weaknesses. In the face of the aloof gods of Avalonia, the men and women of Elaea run amok stumbling and failing. What the poet is suggesting is that these men and women should not look to Jüt as their exemplar, but Flora. For she represents all that the poet longs for in the masquerade of death that he knows as life: valor, honesty, charity, and the ability to chose and act. In this way, it is Eustace who most resembles Flora, but, I would suspect, the poet believes the Umbrian spymaster to be misguided in his desires. It is not that Eustace is corrupt, but that he chooses the one over the many, a choice that Flora with her crocus would most certainly never make.

In the end, I submit that Flora is the prime actor in the poem and, as such, the archetype by which all Elaeans should measure their actions. How does this change our reading of *Sigurd's Lament*? The poet creates a world that is grim and nearly unbearable. There is betrayal, death, and much hatred. The boots of war quickly trample what little hope there is in Elaea. In the heavens, the situation is no better. The gods fight amongst themselves, are bound by time and fate, and take small interest in the affairs of humanity. So where does this leave the very real men and women of Elaea eking out an existence upon the stern earth? Where does this leave the men and women of Elaea who believe themselves to be trapped by fate and time and, as the poet writes, "the weird?"[53] It leaves them with two things: one, the ability to choose and, two, the ability to

51. Ibid., X:29.
52. Cf. H. B. Peters, *Religion*, and W. W. Peters, *Notes and Letters*.
53. *Sigurd's Lament*, IV:28.

act. For the poet, these dual abilities stem from the representation of the goddess Flora and spill over onto the men and women living on the bleak earth. Humanity can set its own course and act in accordance with its own laws, but only by dethroning itself from the seat of primacy.[54] Simply put, for the poet, anthropocentrism is dead. Should the world burn, then that is only the natural consequence of humankind's selfish choices. Should the world thrive, living out and embodying the ethic represented by Flora, then that too is the natural result of humankind's recognition that they are but part of a much larger universe in which there is no *a priori*, but only a web of complex, transversal relationships.[55] For the poet, that is hope.[56]

Religion and Politics

In my first book on religion in *Sigurd's Lament*,[57] I claimed that religion and politics are complex, rhizomatic systems—narratives, if you like—that can be described as intertwined webs of embodied meaning. Without entering into the reeds of academic theories of religion and religious studies,[58] I do think it is important to make a few claims as to the role that both religion and politics play within *Sigurd's Lament*. Remember, however, that contemporary categories like "religion" and "politics" are modern, heuristic constructions that do not transcend time and space. Our religion is never their religion and our politics is never their politics. Acknowledging for the poet that religion and politics are not stable and separate categories is rather helpful. Whereas we make a complicated distinction between matters of faith and rule, for the poet, religion and politics are mixed categories—theology is politics, politics is theology.

54. Sartre, "Existentialism," 259–73.

55. Braidotti, *Posthuman*, 186–97.

56. Aimless, *Letter to a Drunk Scott*, 654–732.

57. H. B. Peters, *Religion*, 87.

58. Cf. Geertz, *Interpretation of Cultures*; Asad, *Formations of the Secular*; and Orsi, *Between Heaven and Earth*.

Before you climb your high horse and proclaim that ignorance is inherent within the cultural framework of the poet, remember that we do the same. We pretend that our system separates religion and politics. In doing so, we make religion a private affair—a necessary, if blinding move within modern, liberal, and capitalist democracies. We then move through the world professing that our religions have nothing to do with our politics. The poet of *Sigurd's Lament*, however, could not and would not make the same claim. For him, the one directly affects the other. Alfred rules because Jüt has made it so. Egil is wrong, though oppressed, because he moves against the structures previously established by Jüt. Religion and politics are inevitably entwined.

The poet, interestingly and within this complex religio-political paradigm, fights against the dominant cultural signification of Egil. Whereas his culture tells him that Egil is evil—an enemy of the state and its faith—the poet claims the contrary. Egil is not evil, though perhaps an enemy. The definition of evil, after all, depends upon one's viewpoint, which might or might not be correct.[59] What if, the poet asks, we misunderstand our religion and politics and Egil should not be branded an "enemy" but rather a "liberator?" What if the gods would prefer that we view him as "human" rather than "evil?" These are the very real questions of a poet struggling with his own understanding of his culture's categories.

My father vehemently disagreed with me on this point. He claimed that I was not allowing the poem to speak for itself, but rather bringing my background in religious studies to bear on the poem.[60] Well, so be it! I ask you: what manner of man or woman refuses to allow his or her experiences to shape the way in which he or she reads? "Standing in unison," the poet writes, "stern warriors shout, / call for priests / to conduct a service / in honor of Alfred, / the un-healed king."[61] Is that religion or politics? Am I bringing my background, my expertise to bear on the poem? Or is

---

59. Eco, *Prague Cemetery*, and Eco, *Inventing the Enemy*.

60. W. W. Peters, *Notes and Letter*, 108.

61. *Sigurd's Lament*, II:5–6.

something else at work that we cannot understand from our historical vantage point?

In the end, my point is this: what we call "religion" and "politics" are present within the poem, but not as separate categories. To view them as separate is to misread the poem. Religion and politics for the Sigurd Poet are complex, intertwined, and interdependent categories. This is best represented by Jupiter's question to Alfred: "Umbrians broke / boldly with 'laea . . . / Alfred . . . / allow us to ask: / What wrongs have led / to winter's misery?"[62] This is no benign inquiry. Jupiter is asking that Alfred share of the treaty of taxation with which Egil broke. In other words, the god is asking after politics.

Poetry and Cosmology

My father had one question that haunted him throughout his life. If poetry is "imaginative or creative literature in general; fable, fiction"[63] and cosmology is "the science or theory of the universe as an ordered whole, and of the general laws which govern it,"[64] then my father wondered: can poetry create cosmology?[65] In other words, is Elaea real?[66]

I know what I think. The question is, reader, do you?

The keys to unlocking my father's thoughts on this august matter lay within Edward's prophetic monologue and Sigurd's first soliloquy. In the first, Edward discusses the creation narrative of Elaea. In the second, Sigurd explores the epistemological claims of such a narrative.

---

62. Ibid., V:16.

63. *OED Online*, s.v. "poetry," http://o-www.oed.com.bianca.penlib. du.edu/view/Entry/42251?redirected From=poetry.

64. *OED Online*, s.v. "cosmology," http://o-www.oed.com.bianca.penlib. du.edu/view/Entry/42251?redirected From=cosmology.

65. W. W. Peters, *Notes and Letters*, 432.

66. Cf. Danielson, *Book of the Cosmos*, and Hallyn, *Poetic Structure of the World*.

In Book VI:1, Edwards speaks his prophecy concerning both the past and future of Elaea. "'Twas void of nothing," he begins, "'twas verily at peace . . . / Neither time nor language / exists in stasis . . . / but neither are begotten nor built. / From emptiness then, forged and fashioned, / the Makers created matter and spirit / and form."[67] In the beginning, there was paradox. The cosmos was at rest but still inhabited by both time and language, which necessitates change, growth, and movement. The Makers existed within this paradox and through it created matter, spirit, and form. They created, in other words, that which Jüt would later use to create the multiverse.

The language he was given, however, was not the first speech, but rather that which inaugurated the spacetime continuum we know. In the beginning then was language and word and thought. This is not, to be clear, the linguistic bondage of structuralism. Whatever language was used throughout the earliest epochs of Elaean cosmology was fully embodied. "Sign and referent," the poet writes, "were sown in synthesis."[68] I can only describe this as *Being*, and it was this *Being* that my father believed poetry created.[69] How?

"Nothing . . . is natured benign," the poet writes, "but granted choice for good or ill."[70] The poet, according to my father, takes that which is neutral—language—and from that constructs a world filled with the living. As a caveat, it is important to note that I disagree with my father, insofar as claiming that language is never neutral. Perhaps the paradoxical language of the Makers was, but our language always leaves someone or something transgressed. Language chooses and shapes and manipulates the subject. My father refused to acknowledge this, but I believe that the Sigurd Poet did.

"My soul quakes," young Sigurd speaks,

---

67. *Sigurd's Lament*, VI:1.

68. Ibid., VI:3.

69. W. W. Peters, *Notes and Letters*, 34.

70. *Sigurd's Lament*, VI:1.

"when I went to war I rode in anger.
I bumbled through battle as a bringer of death.
I hacked and hewed and Hel I wrought,
but now I find my father buried
and in his place I will be placed.
Such sickness is sought in the slicing melee,
a wrath revealed in the wonderment of
        cosmos.
    Philosophers play
    at unknotting knowledge,
    but by that betray
    our constructed collage.

"For this is truth, terrible and yawning:
all we mold and pretend to master
is the present matter, a primordial motion
crashing and clanging and canceling progress.
We pretend and profess that history is pointed,
but victory is random and rarely righteous
and to rule is to descend into deeper deceit.
But who am I to reject with ambivalence
      the honor
    brightly bestowed
    by great Gotland
    and that freely flowed
    from honest hands?

"I am no king, yet crowned I am.
I am no leader, yet learned I am.
I am no tactician, yet told I am
that my bold blueprint bore the day.
So with these words I readily wield
I must worry my way towards true awareness.[71]

In Sigurd's eponymous lament, I see three things worth noting. One, knowledge is a construction through which one can never break. Two, the poet cannot create anew, but only and forever through preexistent matter. Three, though we are shaped by both language and experience, it is only through the present—bound

---

71. Ibid., XII:2–4.

and mediated as it is by spacetime, language, and experience—that we can approach awareness or meaning.

In the end, yes, the poet creates worlds, but worlds shaped from a preexistent cultural encyclopedia that comprises all we know or have ever known and all we have experienced or have ever experienced. While my father wanted to believe that the poet had a direct connection to the gods, forms, or *Being*, both the Sigurd Poet and I disagree with him. All that we have to construct our world is that which we already have to hand. What is true of the carpenter is true of the poet. And yet, as I write this I want nothing more than to believe, along with my father, that Elaea is real—a cosmic vessel drifting somewhere alongside the Elysian shore. But it is not, and we are forever locked within our own dimensions.

WHY IS NARRATIVE?

In the last four sections, I will do my best to present my father's academic work surrounding *Sigurd's Lament*. It has heretofore gone unpublished.[72] His main concern was seeking to understand the very real and necessary human process of meaning creation. "We need significance," he used to say. "Without it, what are we but worthless sacks roaming the planet, digging trenches, and murdering?"[73] As has already been discussed, my father's pursuit of meaning was rooted somewhere in the trenches trailing throughout the continent. He rarely, however, discussed his WWI experiences. I do not know fully what happened to him, but I believe it was altogether horrendous. I will say no more on these matters. What has been said is sufficient. His experiences affected him and his relationships with both my mother and me.

While my father's work went unpublished, he extensively outlined his thoughts and even went so far as to write an abstract. I will here reproduce the abstract and then do my best to reconstruct

---

72. Cf. Appendix A and Appendix B, where both my father's unpublished paper and bibliography are reproduced in whole.

73. W. W. Peters, *Notes and Letters*, 561.

his argument. You must remember, however, that his academic work is contingent upon *Sigurd's Lament*. The two are not separate.

> *Utilizing Augustine's conception of distention as it applies to memory and time, I explore both the possibilities and implications of applying distention to literature, herme- neutics, and meaning-making practices within religious communities. My contention is that any given text at any given point in its history moves both backwards and forwards in chronological time, causing a distention of reception. In this way, all texts have both before-texts and after-texts that shape the way in which any particular text is read. I show in detail the process of distention within a subjective-objective reader and a subjective-objective hermeneutical community. Having established the work of distended reception and its bloom in both time and space, I then turn to exploring its implications for both meaning- making practices and hermeneutical communities. Par- ticularly, I show that the process of meaning-making is rooted in the development of what I call, "hermeneutical clusters"—a fluid and dynamic gathering of texts through which individuals and communities make meaning. These clusters are indicative of both the boundless nature of meaning making and the game of hermeneutics—the seemingly arbitrary rules that a given community estab- lishes based upon their hermeneutical cluster. The dual ideas of distended reception and hermeneutical clusters are a call for seeking to understand both the other's embod- ied position and meaning-making practices in a multivocal and, at times, polarizing world.*

—W. W. Peters, Abstract, 1932

Social World Turned Story

Having combed through his notes, I have previously shown that this abstract was the beginning of a long process for my father. He sought to add to it, but was never able. At the beginning then, it is important to recall a few things. One, the process of meaning creation that my father was at pains to show was contextual. It must be read against and within the philosophies of spacetime, big history, and posthumanism. Without this context, my father's work on distention is greatly limited. Two, narrative or "the injected narrative" is itself not meaning, but rather a necessary condition for meaning. Three, religion was integral to my father's search for meaning. It is important, therefore, to understand the way in which he used "religion," "meaning," and "religious meaning."

One, in the beginning was the big bang. We know little more than this, but we do know that at that moment the cosmos was "created." From there, it grew ever outwards, cooling and forming. Sun. Earth. Moon. Humanity. A humanity that will eventually die or evolve or morph into something wholly new. According to my father, however, the cosmos will always *be*—expanding, growing. Who are *we* in the face of such power?

Through this lens of space and time and big history, my father arrived at posthumanism, which dethrones humankind from an anthropocentric understanding of reality. In other words, the cosmos is vast, humanity is small, and we are not its center. In the face of such overwhelming insignificance or infinity, my father often wondered, how do we arrive at understanding or approach meaning? How do we live? This was his life's work spilled out in the form of *Sigurd's Lament*.

Two, in order to arrive at meaning, humanity must inject a narrative into its experience. This narrative could be empirical science, enlightenment humanism, Christianity, or even the present conception of Western Human Rights. The narrative itself does not matter. What matters is that in order to confine the universe's expansion—and humanity's place within it—humanity must inject an *a priori* narrative into its epistemology. This narrative, whatever it might be, does not itself constitute meaning. It is, rather, the necessary condition for it. "The observer," theoretical physicist, John Archibald Wheeler writes, "gives the world the power to come into being, through the very act of giving meaning to that world; in brief, 'No consciousness; no communicating community to establish meaning? Then no world! . . . The universe gives birth to consciousness, and consciousness gives meaning to the universe."[74]

Three, my father defined religion—rightly or wrongly—as "the practice and celebration of a collective narrative, which breeds either a social or particular identity and allows one to order his or her world." Religion then is all that which rises up and enters into a complex web of relationality with a particular community's injected narrative. It is this complex web or hermeneutical cluster circumscribing an injected narrative that allows for meaning. But what is "meaning?" As my father defined it, "meaning is interpretation."

> It is the interpretive process by which one seeks to create understanding in his or her world. Experiences do not happen in some perfected and detached reality. There is no objectivity. Everything we encounter, we make sense of or interpret. This ongoing process of meaning making or interpretation is a dynamic interplay between communities, individuals, and the experienced world. It is both encyclopedic and rhizomatic. Nothing we experience is linear or clear or progressive. There are only particular instances or moments of experience that require a connection to be made between our cultural encyclopedia and our embodied reality.

It was important for my father to connect these two ideas. Why? Because his understanding of "religious meaning" ultimately both was rooted in his reading of *Sigurd's Lament* and laid a foundation for his dual academic ideas of distended reception and hermeneutical clusters. On a small scrap of paper tucked inside his copy of Tasso's *The Liberation of Jerusalem*,[75] he wrote:

> Can I merge my two definitions of both religion and meaning and approach, ever so humbly, a preliminary definition of religious meaning? No. Whatever my definition, it will fail. Both our language and our semiotic fields bind us, much like the prisoners chained within

---

74. Patton and Wheeler, "Is Physics Legislated by Cosmogony?," 538–605.

75. Tasso, *Liberation of Jerusalem*.

Plato's cave. We can never fully approach, with any real comprehension, reality—no matter how abstracted. But should we not try? In that light, I offer you, Tasso, this definition: religious meaning is the embodied hermeneutic through which one engages his or her world. In other words, religious meaning is the process of embodied interpretation utilizing the absolutizing lens of religion.

Whether or not you agree with my father, it is important to note these definitions and models before entering into a more robust engagement with his academic presentation of *Sigurd's Lament*. For him, one could not read either the poet or the poem aright without understanding it as a religious narrative, constituting meaning for its particular community. It is not a dead text, but rather a living and breathing and dynamic cultural artifact that at one point in time created the world for both its hearers and readers. In other words, the poet looked out into the vast sea of writhing motion and wrote *Sigurd's Lament* to inject a narrative, an *a priori* necessary condition, by which his community could construct meaning.

DISTENTION'S BLOOM

My father was an avid reader. He would wake up at five every morning, enter his study, which was a wash closet off of the kitchen, and sit in his small, leatherback chair. He would read until seven-thirty and then make breakfast—potatoes and eggs. Sunday through Saturday, it was always the same routine.

He did not limit himself to one genre or style of writing. He only loved to read, so he read it all. In this way, he came across the concept of big history, "the approach to history in which the human past is placed within the framework of cosmic history," from the beginning to now and into the future.[76] He later told me that this was the impetus for his life's work. He was staggered by the

---

76. Spier, *Big History and the Future of Humanity*, 1.

thought. Growing up when he had, "man" was at the center of the universe. "But what if," he often mused, "what if man is not?"

This question led him into all manner of scientific exploration, but particularly into the field of theoretical physics. He was intrigued by the idea of understanding human history not from the birth of civilization, but rather from the great explosion instigated by the big bang. This, of course, led him to Einstein's relativity, quantum mechanics, string theory, and Marcelo Gleiser's asymmetry.[77] The ideas that time and space could be manipulated and that uncertainty was at the heart of the universe were almost too much to consider.[78] For him, *anthropos* was at its end[79] and what was needed was a radical new vision for the human subject, wherein the self or the "extended self" was understood in connection to animals, the planet, and the emerging technologies of the modern era.

In the end, he was overwhelmed. History was new. The universe was expanding. And the human subject was a problematized, jumbled mess. My father's sincere desire was to understand how humanity could move forward in light of these revelations. For him, *meaning* was at the center of the academic universe.

What follows are my father's thoughts on a new kind of human understanding or meaning construction. Though I will write them in such a way as to avoid the cumbersome need of endlessly reproducing "my father," they are his ideas and not my own.

Distended Reception

We are caught in the inescapable present. What is future slips by into that which is now past. As we reach for or grasp after fixed points, we find ourselves stretched thin, trying to remember. But the present consciousness is pulled in two directions—future and past—stymieing us at every turn. When our attention is on the

77. Cf. Greene, *Elegant Universe*; *Fabric of the Cosmos*; and *Hidden Reality*.

78. Gleiser, *Tear at the Edge of Creation*; *Island of Knowledge*; and Rubenstein, *Worlds without End*.

79. Braidotti, *Posthuman*, and Herbrechter, *Posthumanism*.

present "the future is transferred to become the past."[80] Imagine
a person singing a hymn. The hymnal lies open before her. The
music plays. She begins. Earnestly doing her best, she focuses
on what is to come but only within the context of holding in her
mind what has past. In this way, the present flows without her ever
having grabbed ahold of it. As Augustine of Hippo described this
sensation: "A person singing or listening to a song [s]he knows
well suffers a distension or stretching in feeling and in sense per-
ception from the expectation of future sounds and the memory of
past sound."[81] But suppose this is not only true for singing? "It is
also valid," Augustine continues, "of the entire life of an individual
person, where all actions are parts of a whole, and of the total his-
tory of 'the sons of men' where all human lives are but parts."[82]

The difficulty with distension is that it makes us extremely
uncomfortable. We want to believe that we are the masters of our
own time and place, that we have set boundaries that allow us to
know things and engage reality. But this is simply not true. We
are slaves to time and distension, and all that we know—all of
our knowledge constructions and disciplines—are heuristics for
a grasping humanity. In the face of such overwhelming expansive-
ness, how do we begin to make sense of our existence? How do we
begin to construct any worthwhile meaning?

If distention is valid for an "individual person," then it is
equally true for the narratives and texts that function as the focal
points of our lives. Distention is helpful because it allows us to
engage texts in new, fresh ways, ways that instigate the processes of
meaning construction. But what is an Augustinian distention when
applied to literature? Simply put, it is the study of first isolating a
text and then examining how it is stretched in two directions—the
past and the future. To take the *Aeneid* as a representative example,
we know that it entered into the genre known as epic poetry. We
know that it came after the *Iliad* and *Odyssey*, but before *The Divine
Comedy*. We like to believe that there is a nice and tidy chain of

80. Chadwick, *Saint Augustine: Confessions*, 243.
81. Ibid., 245.
82. Ibid., 243, and Psalm 30:20.

48

receptive influences running through time from one to the other. But if we were to look at the *Aeneid* alone, then we quickly see that it not only shapes our reading of Dante, but also our *reading* of Homer, if not Homer himself. The process of distention then is the examination of a particular text's stretching into the past and the future, it is exploring both its before-texts and its after-texts, and the way in which the past (Homer), present (Virgil), and future (Dante) are all in mutual relationship with one another.

By way of contrast, reception theory studies the way in which a text has been received throughout its history. For example, we can research how the Christian Bible was understood or received in fifth-century Rome, which is, of course, a different understanding or reception of the Christian Bible than in twentieth-century America. We are comfortable with making claims that texts move down the corridors of chronological history. "The literature of the past," it is often said, "can always be active in that of the present."[83] But what if a text distends? What if it moves out into both the past and the future, rearranging our understanding of the text or texts? If we can say that the past directs the present, then perhaps we should also admit to the present altering the past.[84] The idea of distended reception reminds us that while texts have historical locations, they are not only historically located. They move out in two ways, engaging the past and the future, their before-texts and after-texts. In other words, texts are always in the process of being consulted, engaged, and redrawn in a process of distended reception. My reading of Virgil shapes my reading of Dante shapes my reading of Homer shapes my reading of Virgil.

This is quite similar, of course, to the notion of *intertextuality*, which suggests that "any text is constructed as a mosaic of quotations; any text is the absorption and transformation of another."[85] At first glance, while distended reception is focused on the text and its distention, it is better viewed as seeking to understand the role that a reader, her interpretive community, and the infinite web

---

83. Curtius, *European Literature and the Latin Middle Ages*.

84. Eliot, "Tradition and the Individual Talent," 39.

85. Kristeva, *Desire in Language*, 66.

of textual interconnections *appear* in the life and interpretation of any text. The focus of distended reception is on both the interplay of intertextuality but also the reader and the reading community that brings her or their own collection of quotations.

By now you are no doubt thinking: "Yes, but I've read all this before, haven't I? Wasn't this the Oulipian platform as posited by those French, harebrained schemers?" Well, in two words, yes and no. To focus our point, two claims will be helpful in understanding distended reception. One, literary history and chronological history are not the same; writers and artists partake of a dual chronology. In this new domain of literary history, the *after* may be situated *before* the before.[86] Wonderful! Two, "anticipatory plagiarism" is the idea that those in the past plagiarize those in the future by anticipating their work. In this way, it can be said that Virgil plagiarized Dante—functioning within literary time—even though he came before him in chronological time.

What proponents of this position take for granted, however, is that dual chronology and anticipatory plagiarism is—*de facto*—a function of literature. Distended reception, on the not-so other hand, opens us to the wonderful process of Augustine's distention and, as I will show, reveals the rules or boundaries by and through which any reader interprets. In other words, it shows us *how* dual chronology and anticipatory plagiarism work or function while providing the reader or her community the necessary guidelines for meaning making.

It is here that we must invite other authors of a distended nature into our conversation, as their help—that of tradition's—should be solicited for all such dialogues. Semiotics, according to some, suggest that texts are signs.[87] A sign's *content*, not its *referent*, is its meaning. These content-laden signs are often called "cultural units,"[88] which exist as essential parts of any world-vision

---

86. Bayard, "Anticipatory Plagiarism," 231–50.

87. See n. 135 and cf. n. 136.

88. Cf. Eco, *Theory of Semiotics*; *Semiotics and the Philosophy of Language*; *Role of the Reader*.

belonging to any particular culture.[89] These cultural units are best viewed as elements in a system of other cultural units[90] limiting or further defining any other cultural units' meaning.[91] It is these cultural units that provide us with an interesting (if distended) philosophical background to Augustine's statement: "[Distention] is also valid for the entire life of an individual person, where all actions are parts of a whole, and of the total history of [humanity] where all human lives are but parts."[92]

What does all of this jargon mean? Simply, that once a text exists as a cultural unit it enters into a cultural relationship with other cultural units. It is these cultural units that exist in literary history, move throughout time and space, and shape the way in which we read both the future and the past. Without cultural units, we would have little with which to work.

To add layers of distention to distended layers, the notion of "transtextuality" will move us ever closer to a succinct and definite conclusion.[93] Transtextuality—that million-dollar word—sets the text in a relationship, whether obvious or concealed, with other texts.[94] What is of concern for us, however, are the subspecies of transtextuality known as "hypertext" and "hypotext." By hyper-textuality, one distended author writes, "I mean any relationship uniting a text B (which I shall call the *hypertext*) to an earlier text A (I shall, of course, call it the *hypotext*), upon which it is grafted in a manner that is not that of a commentary."[95] In this view, the later text is a derivation of the earlier text, a transformation of it. What distended reception claims, however, is that the linearity of *hypo-* to *hyper-* works in multiple directions and in multiple spaces. In

89. Eco, *Theory of Semiotics*, 76.

90. Blah, blah, blah.

91. Ibid., 82.

92. Chadwick, *Confessions*, 243.

93. Succinct? Definite? I am not sure that I can make good on this claim. Cf. Gérard Genette, *Palimpsests: Literature in the Second Degree*.

94. Ibid., 1.

95. Ibid., 5.

other words, distention *blooms* outward into a literary history that can neither be accounted for nor controlled.

Distention and Its Conclusion

In summary, a text, once written—or perhaps conceived?—exists as a cultural unit that enters into a complex web of relationality with other cultural units. In this cultural vortex, a text breaks off into literary history and can move either forwards or backwards or multidimensionally within chronological time. This movement is analogous to a bloom—a blossoming or blurring—within multidimensional space. Given any text then, we can arrive at any other text and all interpretations are, though we may not like the implications, equally valid.[96] What I write here is what my father writes is what Virgil writes is what the Apostle Paul writes is what you will write in the future. In my mind, they are all the same. And how you interpret this text is the working out of your bibliography in relationship with your reading community's bibliography. What on *earth* will you discover?

This leaves us, however, dangerously close to the infinite proliferation of meaning that my father lamented in his readings on big history, spacetime, and posthumanism. If the universe is so diverse and overwhelming that we cannot find meaning within it, then what are we to do when our own fixed texts are similarly disrupted?

HERMENEUTICAL CLUSTERS

Against this backdrop of an unknown, asymmetrical universe[97] and a cultural web in which significance is arbitrary, how is meaning possible? Through borrowing two important concepts from ritual theory—the initial act and the subjunctive—we can begin to answer this question. They provide us with a structure for ordering

96. Cf. Appendix C for my father's diagram of distention.

97. Cf. Gleiser, *Tear at the Edge of Creation.*

our everyday experiences that are otherwise random and uncertain and, in this way, are the necessary conditions around which a hermeneutical cluster can arise, inaugurating the rules of any particular community's interpretive and embodying game.

The Injected Narrative

In the beginning was the chaos and the chaos was neither good nor bad. It was only chaos, swerving and colliding. Chaos is, however, meaningless without order, and so a narrative was injected into perception in order to wrest significance from the otherwise pandemonian ether. The narrative is nameless. It has no meaning itself. It is and can be anything, so long as it is injected *a priori* into human experience, whether personal or communal. Some inject their own narratives. Some claim to have it injected for them. "In many religious traditions," it has been said, "[the] initial act is conceived of as being instituted by a superhuman agent . . . Unlike ordinary causal processes which can always be pushed back one step further, such religious series of acts presuppose a starting point. The buck stops with the gods."[98]

To put it differently, we looked out into infinity and were overcome by the terrible expanse of the natural world. It dwarfed our expectations and diminished our hopes of being the epicenter of reality. So we injected an "initial act" into history, in order to fix a point in time by which our experiences could be measured. The narrative, once injected, was a structure to reality and experience that functioned to order the vast chaos of all that was and is.

It is my contention that the injected narrative is not meaning itself, but rather the necessary condition for meaning construction. Without an injected narrative, an initial act, humanity has no way of ordering, measuring, or comprehending its experiences.

Religion, for obvious reasons, is easy prey. Much harder is science. "Wonderful as it is," one theoretical physicist writes, "science is a human construction, a narrative we create to make sense

98. Lawson, "Cognition," 83.

of the world around us."[99] For him, the grand injection of the theoretical scientific community is the "Ionian Enchantment" of oneness—the search for unification as best represented by string theorists. It is a scientific monotheism, if you like, that provides its representatives a fixed point upon which to hang their hat of meaning.

But why pick on science? For two reasons: one, to show that we all inject narratives into our experience, not only the "believer." And two, because it is a thing that we so often take for granted. In our day and age, science and its constituent parts are both god and monarch, creating and ruling over our empirical and economic powers of knowledge. For us, science is *a priori*, foundational, *ex nihilo*. If science in the modern world injects a unifying narrative into our experience, then it reveals our desperate need for order and structure in a life riddled with infinite and proliferated meanings. We cannot escape the drive to inject a narrative against which to measure our experiences.

Injection and the Subjunctive

The interesting thing about our injected narratives is that we approach them as subjunctives, *as if* they were truly the case. "The creation of 'as if' worlds," one scholar suggests, "is a central aspect of ritual action, which we see as necessary for human life."[100] We inject narratives into our experience as a necessary condition for meaning creation, and then we treat them *as if* they were true. Why? Because the subjunctive-injected narrative implies my father's *aporia* at various points throughout his readings: spacetime, big history, posthumanism, and the bloom of distended reception. In other words, the subjunctive state of the injected narrative implies an "overt tension with the world of lived experience."[101]

---

99. Gleiser, *Tear*, 6.

100. Seligman, *Ritual and Its Consequences*, 25.

101. Ibid., 28.

Whereas some apply the subjunctive only to ritualists, claiming, "ritual actions involving order and harmony are only necessary among actors who see the world as inherently fractured and fragmented,"[102] I think that all humanity looks out into a fractured and fragmented world and as a result injects a subjunctive narrative. This injection is a necessary condition for meaning construction. It is, however, not meaning itself.

The Hermeneutical Cluster and Meaning Creation

Throughout this work, I have used the term "hermeneutical cluster," but I have yet to explain it. Now is the hour. A hermeneutical cluster is the particular web of texts that any individual or community wields in order to interpret their chosen injected narrative. It is through the hermeneutical cluster, interacting with its subjunctive-injected narrative, that meaning is created. It is helpful to think of a hermeneutical cluster like a bibliography. It is the grouping of books that you or your community wields in order to make sense of reality. The hermeneutical cluster, however, is a cluster and not a bibliography, and its various texts are not necessarily books. I use the term "cluster" because it implies a web of interconnected, relational, and dynamic connections. I use the term "texts" because it implies any cultural unit that is put into relationship with any other cultural unit.

It is through the hermeneutical cluster that any particular community establishes its rules of interpretation or embodiment—how to both think and live in the world. It is through the hermeneutical cluster that it arrives at orthodoxy, heterodoxy, or heresy, as well as its praxis counterparts. And it is the hermeneutical cluster that allows any community to make sense of the world, yes, but also to define, confine, and other.

The rules of interpretation and embodiment created by any hermeneutical cluster in relationship with any as-if-injected narrative are analogous to the rules of any particular game. These rules

---

102. Ibid., 31.

of interpretation and embodiment are established in scientific communities, in academia, in nation-states, in religions, and, particularly, in numerous Protestant churches. "We interpret and embody this way," they say, "and not that way—not like them. They've got it all wrong." Based on what? On the rules of their particular game constructed from their particular hermeneutical cluster.

"The hermeneutical cluster," my father used to say, "is like a board game. It's like Catan or Diplomacy or Candy Land."[103] If the game's board and pieces are collectively viewed as the injected narrative and the rules comprise the hermeneutical cluster, then the playing of the game or interpretation or interaction between a board, a ruleset, and a community allow for meaning creation and embodiment in the world. The board game can differ from community to community, but so too can the rules, given the same game. Two communities might have the same injected narrative (board and pieces), but as they bring different hermeneutical clusters (rulesets) to bear on that narrative, their games of interpretation and embodiment (their play) will vary. And who among us can claim that the other is wrong? Or rather, by appeal to what metagame can one community judge another?

---

103. W. W. Peters, *Notes and Letters*, 87. My father's metaphor of the board game as a hermeneutical cluster should not be taken too far. It clearly has its flaws and, perhaps, can only be corrected when extended to role-playing game rulesets like *Dungeons & Dragons*, *Numenera*, and *Symbaroum*. Here, the dungeon or game master creates a world out of a system of rules (a code) in which his or her player characters can subjunctively make meaning (or communicate with aesthetic, ambiguous, and self-referential messages). Silly, yes, but what is the difference between the rules or codes by which any community embodies meaning and the 5th edition of *Dungeon Master's Guide*, which is a system of rules or code explicitly and ambiguously (in the sense that Eco uses ambiguity, *Theory of Semiotics*, 261–76) designed to be utilized so that others can make meaning or communicate in an as-if world? In this way, both the *Dungeon Master's Guide* and the *Player's Handbook* become hermeneutical clusters employed in relation to an injected narrative or "scenario." Perhaps this has gone on long enough or, who knows, perhaps there is much that scholars of religion can learn from the table-top gaming community. Cf. Cover, *Creation of Narrative in Tabletop Role-Playing Games*, and Harrist, "Intro to Tabletop Gaming as Ritual."

Clusters, Meaning, and Subject

Hermeneutical clusters apply to communities—as in the above example—but also to individuals. A community establishes a cluster through which to play their particular game of interpretation and embodiment, but so too do individuals. When a person enters into a new community, he or she brings a personal cluster that enters into a dynamic relationship with the community's. In this moment of exchange, both community and individual are likely to change due to this mutual interaction. The self is not a cloistered, autonomous thing. It is, rather, a self in process with other selves. It is extended to the outside, and the outside greatly shapes the inner-subject. "The self," it has been written, "is a multivoiced and dialogical developmental process, implying that self can be conceived as a narrative construction and reconstruction of the meaning of events . . . the self is not a unified construct but rather a differentiated organized diversity of elements."[104] In other words, the engagement of individual with community, and vice versa, results in a dynamic relationship of meaning creation for the subject rooted in the exchange of hermeneutical clusters.

If a church reads the Bible a certain way and I read it another way, then I change the way in which that church reads and interprets its Bible based alone on my presence on any given Sunday. How? By bringing my hermeneutical cluster into a dynamic relationship with that of the church's. I bring mine. They have theirs. And as a result a dynamic interchange take place. They are changed, but so too am I. In this way, meaning is constructed, but the subject is forever altered.

What does this tells us about the creation of meaning? That meaning construction is a plurality in which both the community and the subject lose themselves while regaining a sense of the whole. We are porous beings moving amongst porous monoliths.

104. Hermans and Hermans-Jansen, "Dialogical Processes and Development of the Self," 535.

Cluster's Conclusion

We all inject subjunctive narratives into our experience. These narratives are the necessary condition for meaning construction. Acting upon them as if they were true, we then develop an intricate web of texts that help us to manipulate the narrative. This web—this hermeneutical cluster—allows for the construction of meaning for both the individual and the community.

CONCLUSION

I began this section with the goal of presenting my father's academic ideas for the first time in print. It is my hope that I have not disappointed his memory. After translating *Sigurd's Lament*, he was immensely interested in the process of meaning construction or the way in which a poem could provide its hearing community with any kind of significance. Against the backdrop of theoretical physics, big history, and posthumanism, all he could see was the infinite proliferation of chaos. He knew that in order for humanity to seek understanding, it must first assert parameters around the chaos. The necessary condition for these parameters was my father's notion of an injected narrative acted upon as if it were true. Any narrative, however, is meaningless, he thought, without a hermeneutical cluster through which to engage it. For him, these clusters were dynamic entities—not abstractions—that allowed for meaning construction. In order to show how these hermeneutical clusters came to be and how they evolved within a dynamic web of relation, he developed the concept of distended reception and its bloom. A text moves out into the past and present, separating itself from chronological history, existing as a cultural unit. As such, it enters into the swarming chaos of cultural units that mutually inform and shape one another. Texts are always in the process of being consulted, engaged, and redrawn in a process of distended reception that, over time, creates something like a hermeneutical cluster, which, interestingly, as a whole also distends. Distended reception, in other words, reveals the rules—injected narrative and hermeneutical cluster—by which we play any particular inter-pretive game, not the least of which is the game of life.

If my father had anything to offer academia, then it was most certainly this: distended reception and hermeneutical clusters. For him, *Sigurd's Lament* must and should be read within that context.

Synopsis

In the fall of 1964, I found among my father's notes and scribbles what is most certainly his own fanciful synopsis of *Sigurd's Lament*. What follows is his summary in full, but—reader beware—all that my father recounts is not chronicled in the poem itself. He writes with an imaginary gusto that creatively adds to the story as we have it.

> *The lays of Elaea tell tale of Egil's legions, in the blanket of winter, testing the long held Treaty of Gramarye by crossing the northern border into Sherwood. The wise posit that Egil's breach of treaty was for both the ore-rich mines of the Breton mountains and the warm-water ports of Elaea. Alfred the Great, fearing the treaty's end with the Umbrian, placed his trust in diplomacy by dispatching emissaries to Egil. With haste, Alfred sent his cousin and advisor, Edward the Elder. Upon arrival at Egil's court, Edward was laid hold of and brashly smitten. Thereafter Alfred received Egil's answer from Sherwood: Edward's crimson cloak. In distress over the loss of his kindred, Alfred fell gravely ill. Egil, rather than risk his Umbrian warriors, waited through the harsh winter in Sherwood for Alfred to pass into the Halls of Avalonia, believing, at that time, he could easily march on Caer Pellinore (Caerpel, so called). Unbeknownst to Egil, however, Alfred, in a sickly dream state, ascended to Avalonia's great hall. It was there, surrounded by the music of the once warriors and champions of Elaea, that Alfred and Edward were reunited. Edward recounted and foretold the story of Elaea's past and future. He sung of sorrow; he sung of joy. He imparted to Alfred the ebbing*

light of Avalonia for, in the wake of the encroaching Got-
lander, Avalonia's bright halls were waning. With this light,
Edward implored, Alfred must fly back to Elaea and over-
come Egil.

Winter gave way to spring, and the most delicate of
flowers, the Elaean Crocus, fully blooming, brought forth
summer. Alfred, rising with the Crocuses into a renewed
life, invoked the right of holmgang and challenged Egil of
Umbria. Alfred rode forth on Gareth, his noblest of steeds,
to meet the Lord of Danelaw beneath the summer skies of
Nottingham's plains. Though Egil was strong in stature and
strength, Alfred bravely fought. With dual raiment—the
fabled sword Durendal and the last light of Avalonia—Al-
fred, though taking many fatal blows, struck true and with
last breath bested Egil. Two men—two kings—lay dead
that day in Nottingham—the fate of Kingdoms laid bare
for other men. In the ensuing confusion, the Lord's of Elaea
(the Council of Nine, so called) could not withstand the
lightning onslaught of Sigurd, Egil's son. The day was a blot
on the scrolls of Elaea. Sigurd marched on Caer Pellinore
and proclaimed himself King Sigurd, son of Avalonia, son
of Egil, ruler of Elaea. Sigurd, after establishing his power,
used Elaea's riches to placate the Council of Nine. Sigurd's
Ealdorman advised sowing discontent among the Council,
while keeping their hands filthy with the profit of Elaea's
riches. The Lords remained distracted; Elaea remained
pacified.

A sorrowful song sung in the first spring of Sigurd's
reign recounts the defiling of the Cathedral in Caerpel
when Sigurd placed a marble bust of himself—eagle affixed
to shoulder—on the wooden altar. His defilement was fol-
lowed by three royal decrees, known as the Danelaws:
one, Sigurd was henceforth to be honored as one who
feasts in the Halls of Avalonia. Two, ensuring honor was
properly discharged, a monthly tribute tax was instituted,
and three, a secondary tax, called the Exchange Tax, was
now to be paid on all goods reaped within Sigurd's empire.
These were troubling laws for a once free people.

One year after crossing the Sherwood, Sigurd, longing
for Umbria, removed himself from Caerpel making the
long journey to his estate in Fjonvar. Before leaving, he

established Fafnir, commander of his comitatus, *as consul over Elaea. General Fafnir was given three Marks to both protect Umbrian interests and to foster a certain measure of subservience among the population. Ealdorman Byrhtnoth, known as the Boar, commanded the North Mark; Ealdorman Wulfstan, known as the Wolf, commanded the West Mark; Skald Sturluson, known as the Serpent, commanded the East Mark.*

And so our story begins: the Halls of Avalonia are silent; the Lords of Elaea are entangled in intrigues and quarrels; High King Sigurd, ruling from his golden throne in Fjonvar, demands both worship and tribute; and Elaeans, oppressed and exploited, groan for sovereignty. The lays of Elaea speak of a time, however, when Elaea will no longer be enslaved, a time when the songs of Avalonia will once again smite darkness. The people even now are whispering among themselves.

Book Summary

While I have included the fanciful synopsis of my father's (see above), I have thought it only appropriate to incorporate a far more factual and accurate summary of *Sigurd's Lament*.

BOOK I

After the appropriate epic invocation, the poem begins *in medias res*. Alfred is awaiting the return of his cousin, Edward, from Egil the Umbrian's camp. Edward is killed, however, a rude fact that quickly leads to Alfred's swooning. Crispin, Alfred's captain, is left in charge to decide the fate of Alfred's army. He decides, after much debate, to wait out the winter to see if Alfred will wake from his coma. Should he not wake, then come the spring he and all his forces will attack Egil for breaking the long held treaty between the two nations.

Crispin and his counselors were not alone in deciding their course of action, however. Egil had sent a spy, Eustace, to uncover the doings of Alfred's army. Egil, upon hearing the news of Alfred's swoon, decides to wait out the winter as well. His reasoning is that Alfred will most likely die during the winter, leaving his army helpless. Egil would rather wait for Alfred's death than risk the lives of his warriors. The book ends with the storms of winter raging overhead.

BOOK II

It is now midwinter. Crispin calls his generals once more to the oak tree to ask if they are set in their present course. The generals agree that they should continue to wait for Alfred's awakening and then call for their priests to invoke the gods on their behalf. The priests come, conduct a service, and are successful in awakening Alfred's spirit—though Crispin, his generals, and the priests are ignorant of this fact.

Ascending to heaven, Alfred sings its many praises and then finds Avalonia's gatekeeper. The "grim-hearted escort" leads Alfred to all of Avalonia's nooks and crannies, but is unable to find Edward. The gatekeeper reveals that all who die do not, in fact, recline in Avalonia. The poet does not reveal the reason behind Edward's banishment to Hel, but the gatekeeper does tell Alfred that all is not lost. Should Alfred want to find his cousin, he must brave the fires of Hel. After Alfred proclaims his intentions, the gatekeeper takes him to the edge of Avalonia, gives him Roland's famous sword, and bids him on his way.

BOOK III

Once in Hel, Alfred quickly works his way down to the Grey Gate, Hel's most despicable corner. There he finds Edward enslaved to one of Hel's greatest captains, Anglach the Fate-Bringer. A terrible battle ensues in which Alfred is victorious but grievously wounded, as Anglach had used a poisoned blade to prick Elaea's sovereign. Edward, thrilled at his release, naysays Alfred's doom and begins to drag the king up the long road towards heaven.

BOOK IV

As Edward carries Alfred out of Hel, the goddess Flora begins to make an antidote for Anglach's poison. The poet recounts that Flora has once before righted a mortal's woes—Brimlad the Elaean soothsayer. Too late, however, for at the border of Hel, Alfred's doom overcomes him. Edward cries out to the gods to make an exception, to intervene in the life of mortals, and to save Alfred, the sovereign of Elaea. If they do this, then he swears that his life is forfeit. The gods, though silent, relent and send Aurora to banish the darkness of Hel. Filled with hope, Edward carries Alfred's body to Flora's hall, where he presumably receives the necessary antidote. In the meantime, the gods convene in the Halls of Justice to decide upon the fate of Edward. After much debate between Flora and Freja, Jüt capitulates and decides against holding Edward to his promise. Freja, in anger, curses Alfred and prophesieshis death, but Flora countermands the curse—though Alfred must now die, his death will live in Elaean memory for ages to come.

BOOK V

Alfred is long abed in Flora's hall, receiving the necessary healing to overcome Anglach's poison. While there, he begins to contemplate his role as king and the duties that a monarch owes to his kingdom. Well enough to rise, he decides that he will return to Elaea and end the matter of Egil once and for all. Flora finds him leaving and asks him to wait one more day so that he might feast with the gods before he returns to the world. Alfred acquiesces, enters the feasting hall, and then recounts the breaking of Gramarye's treaty. Jupiter is humbled by Alfred's virtue. As the feast commences, Edward—now soothsayer—enters the hall and begins to speak his doom.

BOOK VI

Edward, speaking to the Hall of Justice, recounts the creation of Elaea at the hands of the Makers, whom wielded sound as mortar and word as brick. It was language that they provided Jüt to fashion the twelve worlds. Elaea was the last world and the pinnacle of creation, but not all was well. Strife arose between Jüt's children and, as Edward recounts, three heroes emerged throughout Elaea's history to save their kingdoms from destruction. Nearing the end of his prophecy, Edward once more recounts the necessity of the gods loosing Alfred so that he might return to Elaea, overcome Egil, and face his true death.

BOOK VII

Jupiter is now convinced of Alfred's course. He releases Alfred to his fate, which he admits is immutable. Alfred acquiesces to Jüt and bids Edward farewell. Edward weeps at Alfred's leaving and so gifts him, Harbinger, his fabled sword. Flora walks Alfred to the edge of Avalonia, tells him that heaven's light is failing, and implores him to work quickly to dispatch the Umbrian. Should Alfred succeed in his appointed task, then perhaps Avalonia's light will continue to shine. Before leaving, Flora gives Alfred a cloak sown with the light of heaven.

BOOK VIII

Alfred descends into Elaea, wakes, and finds himself within his army's camp. Crispin, Alfred's captain, calls a meeting at the oak tree to see if his battlelords are still set in pursuing their course. Marius, Crispin's strategist, claims that Alfred has been too long abed and that now is the time to strike Egil. Crispin agrees and begins to rally the army, but is stopped short as a murmuring whirls through camp. Alfred has awakened! Crispin runs to the command tent and finds his lord awake and in prayer to the gods. Once finished, Alfred calls his army together and rouses them with a hearty speech.

BOOK IX

Alfred dons his armor and rides to the battlefield. Egil sees his adversary moving and follows suit. Soon both armies array at the field of battle and dispatch their respective sovereigns to treat.

Alfred and Egil lament their fates, but decide that it would be best to settle the outcome through a *holmgang* or single combat. The kings then ride back to their encampments to await both dawn and history.

BOOK X

Magnus, Egil's general, and Eustace, Egil's spymaster, sit atop the battle field and watch as Alfred and Egil commence their *holmgang*. Eustace asks Magnus what he intends to do should Egil be cut down and the answer he hears is insufficient for one such as Eustace. He desires freedom and, regardless of the outcome, freedom he shall have. Leaving Magnus, he dispatches a rider to Sigurd, Egil's son, telling him to make haste through Sherwood and to the field of battle. On the other side of the combat, sit Crispin and Marius, Alfred's commanders. Together they decide that should Alfred fall, Egil and Umbria will be released from their tributary obligations. Eustace then returns to Magnus' side and, seeing the outcome of the *holmgang*, murders Magnus and calls his army to battle. Crispin and Marius, seeing the treachery, command the same thing and, despite the efforts of their overlords, the twin armies wade into the melee.

BOOK XI

The battle commences between Alfred and Egil. Before long, the twin sovereigns kill one another. Egil watches as Alfred expires and then crawls to his king, lays his head on his breast, and follows Alfred to Avalonia.

The rider that Eustace had dispatched arrives in Fjonvar and finds Sigurd sitting by his hearth and lost in words. He quickly informs Sigurd that his father is dead and that he is now the Lord of Umbria. Sigurd, at first disbelieving, relents and rides with the unnamed messenger to the field of battle. Before arriving, however, Sigurd has a short encounter with Flora, who tells him that the choice of life or death lies with him alone. Arriving at the battle-field, Sigurd disregards Flora's advice and rides to avenge the death of Egil.

BOOK XII

The next morning, Sigurd reflects on warfare, his father, and his new role as emperor. He wants nothing more than to refuse the title, but realizes that he is no man to reject the tradition of his ancestors. He then attends his coronation and rides into battle once more to overwhelm the city of Elaea. Having successfully taken the city, the poem ends with Sigurd weighing the consequences of sitting upon the throne of Elaea. He decides that for better or worse, it is his responsibility to unite the kingdoms and forge an empire out of blood. As he sits upon the throne, the poet once more invokes the muses and then proclaims a benediction over his readers.

Sigurd's Lament

Book I

---

*Of beginnings and Alfred's swoon over the death of
Edward, whereupon the king descends into dire illness.*

I   Sing, O Bard,[1]
    sit and tell,
    of benevolent hero
    bidding life,
    ascending to Avalonia,[2]
    arising in grief,
    despairing death
    of dear kindred.[3]

1. In line with the epic tradition, the Sigurd Poet (or, the poet) opens with
an invocation. Rather than invoking the muses, however, the poet invokes an
unknown "bard." It is interesting to note that in Book XII the poet exchanges
"bard" for "muse." Make of it what you will, but I believe that the exchange has
more to do with alliteration than poetics. For a concise examination of the role
of the bard or "skald" in Anglo-Saxon culture, see Olsen, *Poems and Prose from
the Old English*, xi–xxii.

2. This is the poet's conception of a Western, Judeo-Christian heaven.

3. The tight alliteration of the first three books have led many to assume
that *Sigurd's Lament* is a compilation of two or more writers. Though many,
there are only two hypotheses worth mentioning. The first is put forth by
James L. Wintrow and widely accepted. His theory is that Books I–III were
written by an early Briton in the first half of the twelfth century and that Books
IV–XII were completed sometime later by the "Revival Poet" during what is
commonly called the Alliterative Revival (CE 1350–1500). Alistair M. Hobson
posits the second theory. It is his minority position that the poem was written

71

2   Sad 'tis sung,
    sorrowfully waxed,
    of Edward's cloak
    crimson stained and
    Gotlander's grim offspring
    Gramarye's truce breaking,[4]
    reaping a doom
    reversed by none.

3   Sing, O Bard,
    sit and tell,
    of Sigurd's actions,
    afterwards wrought:
    of marching on Caerpel,
    of marauders besetting,
    of loved ones low-brought,
    of lurid transgressions.

4   Scribe doth score,
    set in runes,[5]
    the song now sung—
    Sigurd's Lament.

---

at the tale end of the Alliterative Revival by a coterie of poets living in community. He writes: "The fractured and disjointed alliteration, the word choice and cadence, and the roving narrative all point to a collection of writers rather than *a* writer." I will leave it to the reader to make his or her choice, but—full disclosure—my father sided with Wintrow in this most heated of academic debates. For further study, cf. Wintrow, *Cat and Chalice*, and Hobson, *Through the Windows of Poetry*, 37–48.

4. Though much effort has been made to identify the locales of *Sigurd's Lament*, my father understood these locations to have been either variant spellings of various Anglo-Saxon villages or completely fictitious. Cf. W. W. Peters, *Notes and Letters*, 88–92, and Eco, *Book of Legendary Lands*.

5. Even if you were to date *Sigurd's Lament* at its earliest, then you would still not find runes in use as the primary script. It would appear that here the poet is purposefully casting the poem in such a way that recalls an earlier, more primitive era. As my father once quipped, "If runes the poem be, then ruined the poem is."

Drama in mezzo,[6]
midway begun:
"Harken! from Sherwood,
hither a rider breaks."

5 Thus rises royalty,
rides to greet
the somber scout
slowly plodding.
Clad in cold armor
crisply shinning,
the rider reins,
'fore royalty dismounts.

6 "Narrowly 'scaping,
news I bring.
Umbrian's Captain,
king ever-stately,
replied to thy request,
rebuffing diplomacy."
Breathing, gasping,
Alfred's liege breaks.[7]

7 "Come, O Man,
converse now;
expose truly
of Edward's fairing!"
The rider weeps,
wracks and trembles,
speech undone
while sobbing furiously.

6. Here is another common characteristic found in many epic poems—
beginning *in medias res*.

7. Alfred makes his first appearance. It was my father's belief that Alfred
was an allusion to the historical Alfred the Great, King of Wessex, but I believe
him to be mistaken. Alfred is most certainly a poetic representation of the
archetypical king, much like King Arthur or hagiographic accounts of Charles
the Great.

8 Fitfully composed,
he fatefully utters:
"Egil, the Umbrian,
that unfit King,
clutched thy cousin,
cast him down.
The Danelaw's answer,[8]
drafted in crimson."

9 Steadfast Alfred,
of stateliness unmatched,
clasps close his rider,
constructs his speech;
red eyes glowing,
ruby with rage:
"Lies thou tellest,
lovely Edward liveth!"[9]

10 "O merciful King,"
the mastered man quakes,
"Forswearing false speech
faithfully I speak:
Egil yearns ownership,
enticed by ore;
cast thy cousin down,
cajoling thee to war."

8. Egil is, at this point, the antagonist (though he most certainly does not remain so). The poet has already, nine stanzas in, devised four different nomenclatures for this most intriguing of characters. He is equally called: the Gotlander, the Umbrian, Egil, and the Danelaw. Egil is the character's given name and almost certainly alludes to the great Egil of the Icelandic Sagas. Cf. Thorsson, *Sagas of the Icelanders*.

9. Edward is Alfred's cousin. Much has been written on this ambiguous character and his relationship to Alfred. Some have suggested that "cousin" is a euphemism for lover. It is true that both Alfred and Edward have strong feelings for one another, but that which is forged in battle will often result in strong emotions. Who can say if these passions ever filled the cup of action? Cf. Landroval, *Loved and the Lover in Early Modern Poetry*, 163–68.

I I   Shocked and silent,
slumps Alfred to dust.
Wailing his doom,
wishing for vengeance,
the King's cloak tearing,
royal face clawing:
"Thy beloved dead,
barren mine soul.

I 2   "The greatest of men
grievously handled
by a base-lord,
bane of Avalonia."
The King ceases,
composes himself.
Standing he shouts:
"Men of the South,
           stout-hearted warriors,

I 3   "Let us, O people,
a pyre construct
to burn mine cousin's
crimson cloak.
Gods will forgive,
great as they are,
for lacking in lamentation,
a lifeless body."[10]

I 4   Tall, high-reaching,
timbered and sturdy,
'neath the piney-wood,
Alfred piles the pyre
of Edward the Elder,
ever-champion of Elaea.

10. The poet is referring to the pagan practice of cremating the dead upon a blazing pyre. Cf. Fadlan's account as recounted in Steinsland and Sørensen, *Människor och makter i vikingarnas värld*.

Singing in sorrow,
sadly stoking flames.
Above the burning,

I 5   bright and clear,
a visionary's voice ascends—
a vocal eulogy.[11]
Sweet the dirge sings,
serene beginning;
follows cold wailing,
fashioned from sorrow.

I 6   Then King Alfred,
King of Elaea,[12]
shudders suddenly,
steeped in anguish.
Dizzy with dander
directed northward,
o'erwhelmed with rage,
reality relinquished.

I 7   Crumpling to ground,
the King plunges.
Lucid no longer,
lamenting ended.
The King's *comitatus*
carries Alfred;

---

11. Though much more shall be said about the poet's conception of religion, suffice it to say that my father believed this to be an anachronism from the poet's cultural paradigm. As will be seen, the poetic world of *Sigurd's Lament* is often at odds with what was most certainly the poet's Christian worldview.

12. This seems as good a place as any to discuss the fictitious geographical representation known as, "Elaea." What is it? Where did it come from? If the poem can, with relative ease, be attributed to an Anglo-Saxon poet, then why the location Elaea and not England or Britain or Saxony? While I have neither the time nor space to answer these question, suffice it to say that Elaea—or so my father believed—was a fictional analogue to Camelot or Númenor. For further elaboration see my father's *Notes and Letters* or Aimless, *Letter to a Drunk Scott: An Inkling of Hope*, 47.

gently rests him,
so grievously wounded.

18 Alfred's young Captain,
Crispin so called,[13]
gathers his generals
'neath great oak.
"Our Lord t'was lost,
low-brought by treachery—
purposefully pray
for prudent recovery.

19 "The task 'fore us:
triumph in war
or wait wondering
for wounded King?"
Speaks one General,
a grave leader,
"Forswearing far-back,
I follow Alfred.

20 "With winter near,
waiting's unharmful.
If Alfred arises,
awakened come Spring,
ride to war ready
with the radiant sun.
If sleep, however,
should suddenly seize,

21 "ride come dawn,
disregarding winter,
surprise the Umbrians
and surrender to death."
Breton's General ends,[14]

---

13. Clearly a reference to Guy Gavriel Kay's *Sarantine Mosaic*.

14. Are we to take this as a reference to a physical people group or a ficti-
tious allusion to what would have surely been the poet's time and place? The

bids others speak.
The silent-host,
still and mute remains,

2 2   for what hearing
harkened well.
Crispin, clear-headed,[15]
clasps his warriors,
"This 'vowed:
vengeance forthcoming
on enemy eternal,
Egil the Umbrian.

2 3   "Winter or spring,
war is brought;
Alfred arising
or Alfred descending,
swing thy swords
stouthearted warriors,
let heavy-handed hatred
heap woes on Umbria."[16]

2 4   Cheers arise
to christen the pact,
yet not alone
'neath the oak
is Alfred's *comitatus*
while course electing.

---

poet is unfortunately silent and we are left with nothing more than a question.

15. Poetic epithets are commonplace throughout the poem. While they are wielded for the purpose of alliteration, they also serve two additional aims: one, they provide the reader with a clearer picture of each character and, two, they function as accessible pneumonic devices for the original, oral performers of *Sigurd's Lament*. Interestingly, names of each character can and do change depending upon the needed alliteration. For further examples of this common practice among oral performers, see Bernard Knox's introductions to Robert Fagles' translations of *The Illiad*, *The Odyssey*, and *The Aeneid*.

16. This is often referred to as Crispin's Curse. Cf. Marlow, *Curse and Its Properties*, 437.

Spies the Umbrian
sent that day

25 to collect and catch
the cunnings of Elaea.
Swiftly running,
sweet news bringing
to the ears of Egil,
the ever-wary King.
"Alfred in swoon,"
the Scout begins,

26 "laid in comfort,
lucid no longer.
His warriors waiting:
waking come Spring
or death deciding
dumb Alfred's fate.
The choice 'tis set
to trust in rousing

27 "or duel in winter
at death's tolling.
Either Alfred's awakening
or Alfred's retiring."
Grim Egil grins,[17]
guessing at fate,
"Let them linger,
no lasting harm,

28 "wait out winter
will us Umbrians.
Alfred is doomed,

17. This is Egil's first appearance. Here he is depicted as a grinning and taciturn warrior. The poet will reveal in due time, however, the three dimensional nature of Egil's character. It is moments like these that have led Hobson to posit a collection of writers for *Sigurd's Lament*. For a thorough and vigorous argumentation on both sides of the aisle, see Sopkje, "Tides of Poetry in Community," 156.

his fate decided—
passing 'fore Crocuses[18]
push upward for sun.
War will sunder
winter's coldest days

29 "as Alfred to Avalonia
ascends tormented.
In sorrow found
and surprised in ambush,
Elaea wilt be razed
to rot in grief
at mine crowning
and Caerpel's falling.[19]

30 "Great-grisled work
in gathering word.
Thou peerlessly proved
thy paladin-stature.
Purple-hued honor
and heaped rings due,
for thy constancy,
as King, I prize.

31 "Kneel as agent,
as knight arise.
Lands shall ye hold
as Lord and owner
whenever this warring

18. This can only be some kind of unknown, Elaean flower. It has been interpreted allegorically, however, by Hunt, *Crocus for Your Thoughts*, 168–79. Hunt claims that the crocus of *Sigurd's Lament* is not only a flower heralding spring, but also an allegorical representation of Golgotha. While his argument is both interesting and stimulating, my father would have most certainly disagreed.

19. Caerpel is also known as Elaea. At the outset confusing, it is helpful to remember that Elaea is both the country in which *Sigurd's Lament* takes place and also the capital city of this fictitious realm. The poet, again, will wield different names for the purpose of alliterative necessity.

woefully should end.
For strife bears
a sentient arousal,

32 "a cognizant awareness
combat doth bring,
of life and newness—
the living moment—
for history is carved
by heroes alone.[20]
Forthwith shall thee
in Fjonvar's annals[21]
firmly remain."

33 Egil's brave liege,
ever-stern Eustice,[22]
bows his head
before taking leave
into clear-crisp coldness—
the camp before him
busied in action,
bravely preparing for frost.

34 For writhing o'er mountains,
winter's weary clouds
soar o'er Sherwood[23]

20. A main theme that runs throughout the poem, the role of warfare in culture and its impact upon the individual soldier cannot be overstressed. Egil reveals his understanding of war and soldering. For him, it is an instance of great enticement or what we might call a drug. Cf. W. W. Peters, *Notes and Letters*; Hedges, *War Is a Force That Gives Us Meaning*; Qumbestro, *War and Narrative*; and B. J. Peters, *Through All the Plain*.

21. Fjonvar is clearly the poet's obscene and infantile attempt at alluding to Guy Gavriel Kay's *Fionavar Tapestry*.

22. Eustice has been surprisingly neglected in the field of Sigurd scholarship, but it was my father's opinion that both Eustice and fate were the driving forces of plot throughout the poem. While I disagree with him, I will not contradict his authority.

23. Sherwood is obviously a historical location, but also functions in the

swarthy and doom-filled.
Now snow tumbles
terrible and piercing,
its animated journey—
Avalonia to earth.

---

conceptual framework of many mythopoetic creations. What is of most inter-
est here is the poet's use of liminality, the space between warring kingdoms
that was often thought of as both sacred, haunted, or thin. Here the poet is
nodding to a long line of writers and thinkers who highlight the importance of
liminal spaces for both nation-states and religions. Cf. Orfeo's or Sir Gawain's
forest, Tolkien's Mirkwood, Orual's mountain pass, or van Gennep's monu-
mental study, *Rites of Passage*.

Book II

In which the ascension of King Alfred to Avalonia is recounted whereupon he greets the weeping Escort and journeys to Hel.

I Sorrow and sadness
saturate Elaea,
for the king cannot
come dawn arise.
Winter wields
its weary snow,[1]
burgeoning hopes
bleakly low-brought.

2 Crispin, clear-headed,
calls forth generals:
"Midway midwinter,
muddied, dismayed.
Alfred backsliding,
bearing this choice:
charge forth to Egil
champ'ing red paths—

3 "sterling-white snow

1. For the poet's use of weather and particularly snow, see Pettit, "Snows of Sigurd," 87–112.

stained with hardy-hewing—
or renew waiting
'til royalty mends.
What say ye,
warriors of winter?"[2]
General of Arda utters,[3]
gravely leading,

4 "Cautioning temperance,
King will mend.
Time 'tis needed,
time 'tis had.
Let the course
our Lord did set,
when in sorrow
swooned did Alfred."

5 Grunting agreement,
the grim doth cheer.
"Hear, hear," says Crispin,
that captained warrior,
"to the gods pray.
For greatness might sway."
Standing in unison,
stern warriors shout,

6 call for priests
to conduct a service
in honor of Alfred,
the un-healed king.
Incense drifts skyward
as inquiring clerics,

---

2. Crispin is breaking his previous vow to wait until spring and asking his warriors in midwinter if they would like to attack Egil. The answer, of course, is a resounding, "No!" Noel Baumgartner has posed the question of Crispin's loyalty, wondering if perhaps he was not hoping to succeed where Alfred had failed. Baumgartner, "Is Crispin Disloyal to Alfred?," 23–56.

3. One can only wonder: Where is Arda?

garbed in samite,
glitter in emerald.[4]

7 Yet pleas unanswered,
the priests surrender.
Silks removing,
skills mourning.
The honored now slay
a hollow-horned sacrifice.
Blood spouts forth
burning hands.[5]

8 Silence spreads,
slowly permeates.
To the living,
'tis all and naught,
yet, sleepers stir,
as supplications slip
into divine ears,
those deliverers of doom.[6]

9 Alfred awakens,
ascension beginning;
a spirit stirring
now stripped of flesh.
To Avalonia rising,
awaiting judgment;
mortals though see
a man slumbering.

4. This would seem to depict a rather evolved form of religious devotion, but it must be remembered that the poet is projecting his Christianity back onto the pagan world. I cannot help but wonder if this was a longing for or a rejection of the long-dormant pagan practices. For more, see my *Religion in the Life of Sigurd*.

5. This is almost certainly a fictitious creation of the poet's mind harkening back to an imagined Israel as recounted in the Hebrew Scriptures.

6. It is interesting to note that though benign to the actors, the ritual was integral to Alfred's awakening.

IO   Upward pushes
the pale-spirit:
through billowing clouds,
baleful in Yule;
o'er frosty mountains,
fatefully capped;
'bove rising stars,
brilliantly shimmering.

II   A door doth espy
dangling on horizon,
celestial light
encircling pillars,
marble and ivy
molded divinely,
fires burning
'pon friendly hearths.

I2   The welcoming scene
wondrously crafted,
framed with 'scapes
forged from imagination.
Rising mountains,
rolling plains,
and gushing streams
gathered in oceans.

I3   Lovers in play,
lost ones united;
gods at ease
in gardens cultivated.
Loneliness banished,
longing quenched,
and flawless justice[7]

7. Flawless justice? Indeed! If ever the poet revealed his creative long-
ing, then here it is hung out with the laundry. While Plato might be happy at
this heavenly world of forms, the post-structuralist community is most defi-
nitely angered. Cf. Plato, *Complete Works*; Plotinus, *Enneads*; Sim, *Routledge*

forever reigning.

14 Humbled by beauty,
basking in joy,
Alfred to knees
attentively falls
'fore crying out
'mid consecrated beings,
"Naught but vision
now verily seeing,

15 "Avalonia, Avalonia,
aimed I at thee.
Life a wraith—
longing, desire
resulting in strife,
wreaking warfare—[8]
a shadow of truth,
'till now unknown.

16 "Hateful is life
harrowing all,
a cold-frigid mistress,[9]
cruelly stained."
"Harsh words

Dictionary of Postmodern Thought; and Jameson, *Singular Modernity*. Similarly, if you are interested in following the historical trajectory of this vigorous Western debate between the epistemological necessity of first principles and the ontological reality of social construction, then I would encourage you to look no further than Adams and Searle, *Critical Theory since Plato*.

8. Again, we see the poet's depiction of life as warfare. There is much in common here with *The Alliterative Morte Arthure* and that poet's ambivalence towards war, but for Alfred it would appear as if there are no alternatives: to live is to war. Cf. Qumbestro, *War and Narrative*; Göller, *Alliterative Morte Arthure*; Demarco, "Arthur for the Ricardian Age," 464–93; Chism, *Alliterative Revivals*, 201; Nievergelt, "Conquest, Crusade and Pilgrimage," 90; Armitage, *Death of Arthur*; Benson, *King Arthur's Death*; Gardner, *Alliterative Morte Arthure*; and Tolkien, *Fall of Arthur*.

9. For a depiction of women in *Sigurd's Lament*, see N. V. Peters, *Women at Play both Deadly and Dreadful*.

hastily spoken,"
a vaulted voice
verily chastises.[10]

I 7   Alfred starts,
  answers in kind:
  "Harsh words
  for harsh worlds,
  hastily spoken
  however, I deny not.
  Art thou a god
  abiding here?"

I 8   "Nay, not I,
  not a god,
  biding in Avalonia,
  battle ready.[11]

10. We see the poet's influences breaking forth in a manner worthy of distended reception! This is equal parts Virgil, Dante, and Milton. Though the comparisons are obvious, it is important to point out that the poet's "Grim-Hearted Escort" has much in common with Dante's Virgil, but where Virgil could not ascend into heaven with Dante, Alfred's escort cannot accompany Alfred to Hel. Cf. Virgil, *Aeneid*, Dante, *Divine Comedy*, and Milton, *Paradise Lost*.

11. Here are the first hints of what is surely the poet's conception of an Elaean Ragnarök. The poet will return to this apocalyptic event throughout the poem, foreshadowing the day of doom for which the gods are waiting. My father believed, teleologically, that this betrayed a rough, pagan culture that rooted its values in warfare. After all, to have ones history hurtling towards a fated war is not the hopeful ending that Western Protestants have come to accept as *their* teleological end. While this is perhaps true (and it also highlights the dualistic nature of Elaean culture wherein the gods on one side are fighting against the one amongst them who rises up), this "rough, pagan culture" was also able to produce magnificent works of art, *Sigurd's Lament* included. So, in the end, my father's opinion was perhaps a little too stark and best seen in its context as a response to Nazism and its rise in the late 1930s. He would, of course, fight against the Germans in the trenches of WWI and, and I do not believe he would ever find the necessary forgiveness integral to defeating post-traumatic stress disorder. For a more in-depth look into Elaean art and culture, and particularly the Statue of the Weeping Angel, see Dyson, *Art, Posey, and the Magnificent in Elaean Culture*.

'The Gate Keeper,'
'Grim-Hearted Escort,'
mine names
meted proudly."

19 "Why 'grim-hearted'
in so grand a place?"
"'Grim-hearted' am I,
gaunt in soul,
for willed I be
for woeful tasks."
"'Woeful tasks'
and 'wondrous Avalonia'

20 "are rarely spoken
or runed together."
"Mine task 'tis set
to traverse these lands,
to seek and search,"
speaks the gate-warden.
"Traveling Avalonia
'tis hardly arduous."

21 Thus he tells
tales e're-mournful,
of neophytes coming,
newly arrived,
finding no familiars
and firmly rejecting
Avalonia's halls
alight with mirth.[12]

12. An interesting and nonsystematic approach to the Western concep-
tion of hell. Here, the damned choose their fate after failing to find their loved
ones reclining in Avalonia. It must be stressed that this is not the Protestant
conceptualization of either heaven or hell. Whether Avalonia or Hel, the
choice lies with the individual: will she or will she not choose eternal com-
munity? This, however, betrays a belief in the after life as a potential religious
category in Elaean thought, but that need not be certain. The poet here could
be imaginatively creating in the long trajectory of epic poetry or he could

22 "'Tis a done-well duty,
   yet the dutiful lament
   when such sorrow
   suddenly grips divinity."
   Alfred understanding,
   asks in fear:
   "Hath Edward, mine cousin,
   encountered Avalonia?"

23 Grimly turning,
   the Gate-Keeper beckons.
   "Follow closely,
   as few have traveled
   where thee now go.
   Wan Edward's dwelling
   escapes mine foresight
   eventful journeys e'er-telling."

24 The pair traverses
   purpled hills
   'midst the gloaming
   golden forests,
   and 'midst the dawn
   mildly coming,
   white-capped mountains
   and waving plains.

25 The sun now streams
   silent beams
   as the grim Gate-Keeper
   and the grave King
   view in sadness
   the vast ocean,

———————————

simply be stealing concepts from his surrounding culture. Either way, this is
an interesting image of a religious afterlife *and* an archetypical instantiation of
distended reception's bloom. See H. B. Peters, *Religion*, and *Distention and Its
Many Objects*.

cerulean waves
crashing earth.[13]

26 "High and low,
hero looked for,"
begins the Escort,
"but absent mortals
fettered in fear
are far from here.
I cannot attend,
canst only unveil.

27 "A millstone choice,[14]
O mortal King,
which way thy feet
will warily tread:
The Halls of Feasting,
or fires of Hel?[15]
Waiting warriors
or wandering souls?"

28 The stouthearted soul,
as the sun glows
upon vast waters,
vows vengeance black:
"To Hel wilt travel,
to harrowing gates.
Show me, Weeper,
sundered places."

29 "Mortal, I question!
Mead awaits thee,
shalt thou not tend?"

13. The edge of heaven. Cf. Harper, *Cosmology and Its Import*, 356.

14. From my father's *Notes and Letters*: "The burden laid upon Alfred is unyielding, like a millstone slung about his neck. And here he stands on the edge of heaven, the weight almost too much to bear."

15. What a choice!

Speaks the king:
"Edward's doom
doth weigh grossly,
how canst I forego
'claiming kindred?[16]

30 "Nay, do not tempt,
true friend thou art,
for mine course 'tis set,
and thou canst unravel.
Point the way,
and perilously I wilt travel."
"Thou hast chosen,
thy desire clarion."

31 The ghastly Escort
gravely reveals;
the divine intermediary
directs stalwart Alfred.
"Hold," he commands,
"I happily hand
a rune encrusted sword—
receive thy gift."

32 Bowing low
the brave king
accepts the argent sword.
Alfred straightens,
inquiring its name.
Intones the Escort:
"Durendal 'tis called,[17]

16. For the bonds of brotherhood and family in Elaean life and culture, see Reuel, *Bonds of Brotherhood*, 12.

17. In a strange twist, Alfred is handed the very same sword that Sir Roland wielded at the behest of Charlemagne. Either its steel and golden hilt are magical entities capable of transcending time and space (much like Sir Gawain's green girdle) or we have another moment of distention's bloom. I will leave it to the reader to decide, but do not—I implore you!—make up your mind before reading Sayers, *Song of Roland*, and Armitage, *Death of Arthur*.

a deadly device,

33 "an ancient thing,
an old thing—
the bravest carried,
the boldest wielded—
paladins un-wearying
and presaging 'endurance,'
let ardent Durendal
doomfully guide."

34 The King turns,
the Keeper watches:
a mortal man
masters fate
and forges a path
freshly unwritten—
empty of companions
save the ever-enduring,
Durendal.

Book III

The telling of King Alfred's dire quest into Hel whereupon
he meets Hel's demon hound and the ensuing Battle at
Grey Gate.

I To Hel Alfred hastens[1]
harried along
by grotesque demons,
whom by gods discarded.
Black blood spills
burning the ground,
no longer in Avalonia,
Alfred hastens to Hel.

2 Molten and scree,
mourning he walks
as fel-sick beasts
block the way.
Battle hardened,
battle weary,

---

1. For the life of me, I cannot recall if I have already mentioned it or not, but the Elaean Hel is not our Hell. They are two separate entities, neither of which exist or, if they do, they exist in the mind only . . . well, the former might exist as a state of cognitive being, but the latter, no . . . I think not. I find that I am tired and that these footnotes are rather bothersome. And how do you feel about it? Come now! You must tell.

thy kindred cousin
e'er-closer drawing.

3 Dawn vanishes,
devours sun;
hope falters,
fear burgeons.
Clawing and gnashing,
clear-headed torment.
Alfred near swooning,
swarming dark-ilk.[2]

4 His sword he spies
sated in blood,
whispering words recalled
wrought long ago:
"An ancient thing
an old thing,
let ardent Durendal
doomfully guide."

5 Thrusting upward
that fabled sword,[3]
brilliant Durendal
beats back darkness.
Painful howling
permeates Hel,
spawn of demons
suddenly recoil.

6 Quickening pace,
pure-heart advances
to seek and search
sundered places.
Time is forgotten,
a fleeting memory;

2. A rather gloomy place.
3. Wahoo!

long were the days
languishing in Hel.[4]

7 Downward toiling,
devils encroaching,
sweat pours forth
as folly increases.
Wounds wax,
wanes Alfred's hope.
All is sorrow,
all is sadness.

8 A last place looms
long forgotten
where evil is foulest
and ever-increasing.
Grey Gate 'tis named[5]
as grievous hatred
heaping is sowed
'pon slaves fettered.

9 Alfred in stealth
sneaks and crawls
behind a drift,
a bank of scree.
The view horrendous
so vast before him:
a pit of torture
packed with corruption.

10 'Tis hard to tell
and terrible to count,
such damnable deeds

---

4. For a thorough study of time and its conception in Elaea, see Casio, *Time Is Floating*.

5. Another juvenile allusion wherein "Grey Havens" has been subtly changed to "Grey Gate." Clearly, Tolkien was one of the poets greatest influences. Cf. Tolkien, *Lord of the Rings*, and C. Tolkien, *History of Middle Earth*.

detected by Alfred.
A precious soul
permanently scarred
by the heinous activities
of Hel's Captains.

I I Among all deeds,
Alfred's bravest
in that moment
of mortified terror
did transpire.
Durendal held aloft,
grasping at doom,
grim-hearted Alfred

I 2 charges forth
challenging Hel's Hound,
the ghastly guard
in that gross place.
Anglach fate-bringer,
bane of mortals
and champion of Hel,
harkens to contest.[6]

I 3 Defiance rare-seen
in that deadly pit
rouses slaves
readied for death.[7]
Edward among them,[8]
entangled in chains,

---

6. Rival only to Beowulf's attack on Grendel's mother, Alfred is here attempting the impossible. Cf. Tolkien, *Beowulf*; Heaney, *Beowulf*; and Ringler, *Beowulf*.

7. We can only guess at why these humans are prisoners of the Grey Gate and why their death is imminent. Much research has been done to unravel this mystery, but the majority of it is bollocks. The best of the bollocks is Chaff, "Exploration into Anglach's Gate," 34–78.

8. Edward!

cries to King:
"Chief of men,

14 determined death-bringer,
doubt not thy skill
'gainst Hel's splendor,
thy gauntlet worthy:
for in thy task,
though to thee unknown,
Elaea's fate
floats unsung."[9]

15 Viewing Edward
his valiant kindred,
Alfred harkens.
Aloud then cries,
"Mine brother immutable,
a marvel unearthed!
Breathing found,
breathing redeemed.

16 "Thy King and kindred
knowing the price,
wilt gladly in recompense
rive this fiend.
If death shalt bring
mine doom asunder,
then verily 'tis
time to relinquish

17 "mine stone-grasp
on gifted life."
Thus Alfred speaks
'fore surveying his foe:
Anglach, fate-bringer,

9. My father, after translating this portion, noted in his marginalia: "*Abe45sxx8.*" *He who uncovers the mystery of my code shall find.* Curious to say the least.

bane of mortals.
With fangs and hauberk,
high the hound rises:[10]

18 a plated skull,
a putrid odor,
and claws for claiming
conscious mortals.[11]
A sword he bears,
swarthy and hardened—
n'er disarmed,
n'er bested.

19 Then grunting
in guttural tones:
"Alfred, Elaea's king,
kneel 'fore me.
I wilt forebear,
forgive thy transgressions—
become mine thrall
thy life keeping."[12]

20 Answering his foe
Alfred reveals
and brandishes the bright,
e'er-beaming Durendal.[13]

10. For the role of the hound in mythopoeic literature, see Goodson, "A Hound Is a Hound," 231–560.

11. Anglach has much in common with Beowulf's Grendel.

12. My father remarked in his *Notes and Letters*, "I find it thoroughly invigorating that one such as Anglach would demand the whole of Alfred. He has no desire to best him or even slay him. Anglach, rather, wants a thrall or slave, which is to say, someone to pay him obeisance. Not only this, but also I see that Anglach is an active force in the movement of the story, unlike Dante's devil who lingers, frozen in hell. This unprecedented move in epic literature is . . . no, wait . . . I believe that Milton's Satan—that old devil!—desired something similar for the human race."

13. I am reminded of both Roland, near the end of things, blowing his oliphant and the Scythian's sword in Capybara's, *Superbrothers: Sword & Sworcery EP*.

Charging forth,
clear-light aloft,
he hews in hope
yet honored to die.

2 1   Clashing commences,
claws and steel,
armor 'gainst armor,
admirable swordsmanship.
Neither cringing,
neither shying,
both rather bearing
baneful designs.[14]

2 2   Anglach feints,
falls prematurely.
Alfred advantageously pushes,
ploy unseeing.
Up thrusts Hel's hound,
the unresting manipulator,
strikes Elaea's king
calling forth blood.

2 3   Alfred pricked,
he prudently reels.
Life's breath
and life's blood
pours forth,
the folly unmasked—
'tis no mortal blade
but tipped alchemically.[15]

2 4   Harsh laughter
through Hel rips,

---

14. Resembling the final battle between Arthur and Mordred, see Armitage, *Death of Arthur*; Malory, *Le Morte Darthur*; and, for the gluttons, de Troyes, *Arthurian Romances*.

15. Ah! Poison! A common trick played by fiends.

Anglach the fel,
amused, shouts:
"Poison courses,
king, in thy veins.
Death take thee,
by treachery undone."

2 5 The immortal beast
besought with victory,
turns to squelch
the slaves' rebellion.
His back to Alfred,
broad but bare,
'tis naked to Durendal,
n'er failing sword.

2 6 Alfred stirs
stained with grief—
his doom immanent:
"Doth treachery
befit me?
But nay!
King I'm called,
King I am.

2 7 "Crowned in Elaea,
commanding troops,
nobility required,
noble in death."[16]
To Anglach:
"Turn fiend,
thy back is bare,
but thy back

2 8 "I'll not strike.

16. Cf. Christophe, *Nobility in Hel*, 34: "Though the subjective is a subjective fool when undone by hellish construction, we see the deeply disdained but longed for nobility of the monarchy."

Ill treated!
Though poisoned in Hel
and pulled towards death,
though wilting away,
I wilt n'er change.
My last stand,
standing I make."[17]

29   Alfred sick and broken
bolts forward.
Anglach joins him,
anger embodied.
Leaping forth
the fading king
brings bright Durendal
down 'pon Hel's hound.[18]

30   Head from shoulders
hewn grievously
crashes 'fore the King,
conqueror of Hel.
A fabled deed
forever sung:
Anglach, lie-weaver,
low-brought bravely.

31   Screams burst forth,
scattering through Hel.
Anglach's hordes
hurries away,
frightened by strength

17. Utilizing the theories of Pierre Bayard, Rachel Turner will come to say, "The standard of my stance is to standing I make." Cf. Turner, "Is Poetry in Crisis?"

18. As I am sure you have noticed, the poet rarely uses "upon," but rather "'pon." Do not be alarmed by this idiosyncrasy. It is nothing more than alliterative necessity once again rearing its ugly head. Well, that *and* the poetic sound of a thing. If you do not believe me, then try reading the poem aloud. After all, that was the medium for which it was written—oral performance.

flowing in Alfred.
Collapsing, however,
the king lay dying.[19]

3 2   Edward the Elder,
ever-champion of Elaea,
springs forward
flying to Alfred's side.
"'Tis too late, brother,"
the tender King murmurs,
"Anglach's poison
perfectly mixed

3 3   "fulfills its duty."
"Forget thou, King,
Avalonia boasts another
ancient name
bequeathed by gods
born true countless times—
Fortuna Abrogatio."[20]
Foreswearing despair,

3 4   desperate comrades
dark in thought
rise together
to risk the journey
through the unnumbered
terrors of Hel—
arm-in-arm,
armed with hope.

19. A common motif in phantasmagorical creations, Alfred sacrifices himself so that Edward might live.

20. My father rendered this phrase in Latin in order to provide the poem with a sense of the primeval, though doubtlessly it was in some unknown and ancient Anglo-Saxon script. My father's linguistic choice is best rendered as "the repeal of fortune." Edward R. Masterson, however, renders it as "the canceling of fate." Whichever choice you make, the general idea is that in Elaea wondrous things are known to happen and that even being poisoned in Hel is not so bad. See *Notes and Letters*, and Masterson, "Canceling of Fate," 112–43.

Book IV[1]

Of the journey back to Avalonia, Edward's bargain, and the resulting dispute between Freja and Flora in the Halls of Justice.[2]

I Darkness descends
   down dark corridors
   as fated brothers
   falter through Hel:
   The conqueror Alfred,
   king though venomned,
   Edward the Elder,
   ever-champion of Elaea.

2 High above, however,
   in halls gilded,
   One with prescience,
   prepares her potion.

---

1. This is, of course, where Wintrow posits his two-author hypothesis. The reader, no doubt, will not fail to notice the less strict alliteration that follows throughout the rest of the poem.

2. Freja is the Elaean goddess of love and sexuality, but also of war and death. Flora, on the other hand, is the goddess of spring and work, but also wisdom and elegance. The "Halls of Justice" is a synonym for Avalonia or the feasting chambers of the gods. For more, see my *Religion in the Life of Sigurd*, 112.

Renowned elixir
ne'er quaffed by mortal,
save one heroine
in service to gods.[3]

3   Brimlad the doomsayer
by fate brought low,
once drank that desired
and destined brew.
Singer and prophet,
sharp-witted Brimlad,
whom fair Freja mistrusted
for failing gods.[4]

4   Mortals move
through murk uncertain
and jealous gods
judge unjustly.[5]
Gripped by the weird,

3. Ibid. Flora, as the goddess of spring, is also the goddess of alchemy, crafting, and poetry. It is no mistake that she is present in this poem.

4. Brimlad, as the story goes, was an Elaean prophetess serving Flora and overseeing the rites of spring. During one such ceremony, King Deómer III cast her down, overcome by her beauty, and raped her. Brimlad, in response to the offense, called on the gods to doom King Deómer III. Jüt, known as the Stern God, responded by flaying King Deómer III and displaying his body to the monarchs of the remaining eleven kingdoms. The message was clear: not even a king has the right to interfere with the messengers of the gods. Freja, as King Deómer III's divine consort, was angered. There was very little she could do to Jüt, however, so Freja employed the Sicarii of Elaea to assassinate Brimlad. While they were successful, Flora was moved to pity and, breaking the rules of divinity, concocted a formula through which Brimlad could revive. Once recovered, Flora manipulated the seen world in such a way that Brimlad, with relative ease, could propagate revenge. For this interference, Freja and Flora—though two sides of the same coin—became celestial enemies. For more, see my *Religion in the Life of Sigurd* and N. V. Peters, *Sexism in Alliterative Verse*, 104–231.

5. Another feather in the cap of those proponents of the multi-author theory, the poem will, from this point onward, become increasingly philosophical.

great Brimlad fell
undone by men
in unthinking deeds

5 prompted by Freja
to pursue her death.
Fair Flora, however,
forever takes pity
on those serving
theistic avatars.
Potion wrought
poison to counter

6 administered with mirth
by ministers fair.[6]
Anger welled
grievously in Freja,
but Flora fended
the flames well-fashioned.
Brimlad arose
brimming with hope

7 and revenged death
on reapers of doom.
Now enlightened,
numinous Flora,
stoops to task

---

6. It is not that I refused to love him, my father, it is that he was never
the same after returning from the great war. A once genial and quiet man had
become easily irritated and harsh. He increasingly focused on his translation
of *Sigurd's Lament* and, I think, allowed his marriage to suffer because of it.
Imagine my surprise then, years later and after his death, when I decided to
continue that which he stopped. My father had completed his translation, but
had been unable to complete his textual-critical notes and academic apparatus.
There are times, reading his material or pouring over his notes, that I begin
to ponder his legacy. But he is gone, and I am not. He once said to me after
he had been drinking and staring too long at his life's work: "War is eternal,
Hawthorne, but so are words." How the mind wanders.

with stern expression.[7]
Elaea, she's learned,
lingers in balance

8 should stout-hearted Alfred
suffer Anglach's spell.[8]
Mending and reaping,
the Maiden mixes:
a horn of mercury,
a spar of hellebore,
and flowers of Aeris
for our fallen king.[9]

9 Returning to heroes
together climbing
up Hel's mountains
protruding in limbo.
"Nay," cries Edward,
"night prithee scatter.
Alfred must find
Flora's gilded halls."

10 Groaning in arms
greatly holding,
Alfred reflects
on fleeting life:
"Lo! Limbs fail
lords and peasants.
Ne'er surprising,
Never exempted.

11 "Death deals all

7. Having once made a mortal's potion, Flora is condescending to once more fashion something anew.

8. For further insight into a king's relationship to his land, see Lee, *Hamlet Sheared*, 33–54, and Helvig, *Royal Court in Poetics*, 203–26.

9. Though many have tried, none have tracked down the exact ingredients of this potion. Aeris is an unknown solvent.

dreadful wounds.
To weep and wail
'tis wearily our lot—
rest resolutely eludes
royal flesh."
Swooning in anguish,
sovereign Alfred sleeps.[10]

I 2   "Nay," cries Edward,
"night prithee scatter.
Lord thy shelter,
I long to find."
Fiends of Hel
find our brothers,
too late their leave-taking,
too late their escape.[11]

I 3   Trapped by fire,
trampled by hounds,
Edward calls forth
dim and dreary,
on the edge of 'Ionia,
the justiced realm:
"Gods hear me,
great and goodly,

I 4   "burdened with blood
mine veins betray
him whom I love—
lord and master.
Hel's star dim
circles thy heavens
splashing darkness
in 'saken realms.

10. He seems to do this a lot.

11. My father once told me that this was his favorite scene. His affinity
for this section, no doubt, was more about his fighting on the continent then
about *Sigurd's Lament*.

I 5   "Cans't thou view
a cloven future
in omniscient minds
magnificently immortal?
Should Alfred die,
die then history—
Elaea wilt suffer,
thy lands created."[12]

I 5   Edward the Elder,
Elaea's champion,
rests his head
on regal chest.
Crying out,
calls forth Edward:
"Thy light for life!
Languish I wilt

I 6   "in Hel's dark prison.
Redeem Alfred.
Reveal thy way.
Raise Aurora.
Let dawn's light
illuminate Hel."[13]

12. Poetics and historiography traditionally go hand in hand. This can best be seen, I think, in Virgil's *Aeneid* and that poet's desire to not only rewrite Roman history, but also to connect it to a deeper, more ancient tradition. If there is anything like an Elaean historiography, then it is most certainly revealed here. The gods are outside of time in such a way that they posses middle knowledge or the knowledge of all that *could* happen. For one particular iteration of history, Alfred must live, if only for a time. Edward's crude question asks the gods to not only decide, but to decide now. For to wait, for Edward, is tantamount to a sin of omission. Interestingly, Edward claims that Elaea's history is wrapped in its relationship to its king, in this case, Alfred: "Should Alfred die, / die then history." A stark claim that history can and will end before its time should the gods refuse to act. For more on poetics and historiography, cf. Adams and Searle, *Critical Theory since Plato*.

13. This is commonly referred to as Edward's gambit. Cf. Macavoy, *A Cousin for a Queen*, 8–31. Aurora is the goddess of dawn.

The Elder deems
all is done,

17 an' closing his eyes,
countermanding hope.
Twice it was
in time so short,
bending the gods
benefited their heroes.[14]
And Lo! From east,
lingering no longer,

18 dawn's brilliant star
stretches its fingers.
Rising, reaching,
radiance crests
the horizons of Hel
hovering in dusk.
Gently caressing
our great heroes,

19 Aurora banishes
the banes of Hel.
Edward the Elder,
Elaea's e'er-champion,
seeing dawn's light,
sings with hope:
"Up, up, arise
mine proud lord,

20 "the gods have lent
their great light."
Sweeping Alfred,
swooping from dust,
Edward installs
desire from doom.

14. The first time being Brimlad. "In time so short," however, is doubt-lessly from the perspective of the gods.

"Mine bargain made,
mine bargain keeps"—

2 1   'Tis true in 'Ionia,
'tis true in Hel.
Edward vows
to doom his life
in return passage
for stouthearted Alfred.
As the border nears
between hea'n and Hel,

22   gods are greeting
in great council hall.[15]
"Aye!" Freja screams,[16]
"forsworn 'tis life.
Edward the Elder,
Elaea's champion,
has cast his eyes
in confusion and doubt.

2 3   "Have we not,
we vaunted few,
dealt such doom
when deemed true?
Fair Orpheus failed
when fate he trialed
without gods consenting.[17]

---

15. For the first time, the perspective will shift away from Alfred. Here we
will receive a rare and precious gift, a peak into the world of the gods.

16. Freja will demand justice. She wants Edward's life. There is no doubt
that she is here remembering the Brimlad episode.

17. Time is collapsing on our narrative. Freja discusses the Orpheus myth
as if it were an Elaean mythology and not a Greek one. The decision to take
Eurydice from Orpheus was the gods' choice who now abide in the Avalonian
Hall of Justice. The precedent, according to Freja, has been set and should—
when measured against the ideal—be maintained. Eurydice was lost at Or-
pheus' transgression, and likewise Edward should now be condemned to Hel
for the bargain that he struck. The implications for mythology and literature

Grievously we judged

24 "his backward glance
belying Eurydice.
How now! Should we,
we numinous and vaunted,
our wills bend
when our hearts break?
Nay! Laws are nothing
'less maintained."

25 Applause proceeds,
produced by Freja,
circling round
uncreated halls.[18]
Flora, in fair anger,
flings herself upright
and demands divine
minds give audience.

26 "Orfeo," Flora whispers,[19]
"into Faerie waded,
found fair gods
and fair wages.
Gathering Heurodis,

are staggering. Freja's claim insinuates that literature is not a chronological affair separated into neat, little categories of reality, fiction, and fantasy. For Freja, rather, that which happens in literature is accessible across time and space. In other words, there is nothing that separates Freja's reality from Orpheus' or even mine. Perhaps, you are thinking, the purview of gods is not that of mortals. But I would argue by claiming that literature is as much mortal as immortal and that, in the playground of literature, even mortals are gods. Cf. Bayard, *Anticipatory Plagiarism*; Bulfinch, *Bulfinch's Mythology*, 185–88; Hamilton, *Mythology*, 138–42; and Ovid, *Metamorphoses*, 339–67.

18. Are the Halls of Justice *a priori*?

19. Wonderful indeed! Flora counters Freja with a different but similar Orpheus myth, the Anglo-Saxon tale of Sir Orfeo. In this myth of Faerie and the like, the gods relent and allow Sir Orfeo to reclaim his wife back from the Faerie King. Flora's counterargument is that the gods having once relented should, in Edward's case, do so again. Cf. Tolkien, *Sir Gawain*, 129–45.

this great king
returned to temporality
having tempted fate.

27 "The exemplar set,
Zeus cannot renounce[20]
the very justice
we 'vaunted' established.
Forgo error
and forgive audacity,
Elaea needs its king—
its king needs Edward."

28 Standing in terror,
uttering the weird,[21]
Jove pronounces
his just judgment:[22]
"Rarely doth gods
recognize mortals,
flitting and flinging,
frail and uninteresting.

29 "Yet strangely now
a stirring surfaces,
wells within
my well-worn heart.[23]
Devotion so dutiful
to divinity 'tis blind.
But conquered Alfred,

20. See my *Religion in the Life of Sigurd* for a discussion on the many names of Zeus as employed by the poet.

21. "Weird" in *Sigurd's Lament* is best understood to mean either "doom" or "fate." Cf. Morris, *Well at the World's End*, or any other Morris text. Truth be told, they should all be read, again and again and again.

22. The high god of the Elaean pantheon speaks. I suggest that you listen.

23. See my *Religion in the Life of Sigurd* for a discussion on the way in which the Elaean gods can be emotionally manipulated to right a wrong, a wrong so perceived by mortals.

king and venomned,

30 "and Elder Edward,
Elaea's e'er-champion,
art heralded heroes
heartily born.
Grievous their death
and grimly dolled,
we shalt forbear
shuttering their souls."

31 Surprised by justice,
erect she stands:
"Doom thou wrought,
delaying wrath.
Elaea shall fall,
and feebly languish."[24]
Freja now finished,
flees from Valhöll,[25]

32 but not before
arboreal Flora,
mitigates that which
malice sought.
"A song once sung,
sows melodies deep.[26]
Laboriously I formed
'lixir harmonious.

---

24. From my father's *Notes and Letters*: "Freja cannot abide Zeus' ruling
and storms out of his presence. She is, no doubt, recalling the Brimlad affair.
Her curse, however, will linger on throughout the poem and eventually cost
Alfred his life," 86.

25. "Valhöll" is a variant of the Norse "Valhalla" and clearly another name
for the Avalonian Hall of Justice. See Magnusson, "Valhöll in the Life of a God,"
234–58.

26. Flora is, through an analogy to music, able to mitigate Freja's curse.
In this way, Alfred will still have to die, but his death will be the cause of a
greater good.

33 "Perhaps I'll find
in fickle Freja
a royal refrain
to repair such ruin.
This I command,
this I chant:
Alfred returned,
restored to life,

34 "wilt deem death
no docile foe.
Slain he shalt be,
surrounded by Umbrians,
but as exemplar
bravery shall propagate
from whence shall rise
a future hope."[27]

27. What this future hope is one can only guess. But the idea or concept of a *rex quondam, rexque futurus* has a long and storied tradition. Cf. Aland, *Greek New Testament*, White, *Once and Future King*, and Malory, *Malory: Complete Works*.

Book V

How Alfred is healed by the works of Flora, his entrance into the grand feasting hall of Jove, and his recounting of the breaking of the Treaty of Gramarye by the Umbrian, Egil.

1 Long Alfred lays
lingering abed
in halls of healing
humbly brought
by Edward the Elder,
e'er-champion of Elaea.
Flowing from Flora,
fair goddess,

2 her bright elixir
engulfs his wounds,
cajoles Alfred,
king stouthearted,
to vigor and strength,
and a sturdy vitality.
Long he lays,
lingering abed,

3 dwelling on 'laea,
his doomed domain.

Sighing and singing,
he summons his lore
and explores dim paths
exhibited by woe.
"Now recovered,
neglecting death,

4 "having rescued
honest Edward,
return I must
to royal duties.
No longer to linger,
lying abed,
to Elaea I fly,
towards my fate—

5 "tomorrow I go,
tarrying no longer."
"Hark," he hears,
hushed and somber,
Flora is speaking,
fair and true:
"Death awaits
in deeds undone,[1]

6 "if thou must flee
first partake
in banquet splendid
by gods arranged—
destiny waits well
for wondrous divinity."
Having heard
hard words said,

7 Alfred deems

---

1. Alfred has no recourse to escape his fate. He must die in order for Elaea to live.

the day will wait.[2]
Rising from rest,
royal-Alfred stands
and presents himself
poor and humbled
'fore the gods
in their fabled feasting hall.

8 Long tables
laboriously set
stretch with joy
in justice's hall.
Mirth and merriment,
moods of feasting,
waft in assembly
attended by gods.

9 Linen golden
lays on tables,
worthy arrangements
for wisdom so great.
Kindled incense
kites the air—
drifting, gliding—
delightful odors.

10 Holly sprinkled,
hewn from branches,
rests so regal
round the room.[3]
Surrounding the hall,
statues and ornaments,
such that mortals
would swoon to see.

2. For more on banquets and the gods' ability to delay divinity but not fully overcome it, see Harriman, "Gods at Play and Dying," 67–89.

3. Holly, or *lex aquifolium*, symbolizes truth. In the Hall of Justice, it is not amiss.

I I Fires art lit
framing the feast,
aura of heaven,
honeyed and sweet.
Mead is poured
moist and pleasing,
as lyres play
lustrous melodies.

I 2 Alfred stumbles
surprised by entering
into company
crowned superior.
"Who am I,
a worthless man
opaque and crass
presuming to infiltrate?"[4]

I 3 "A guest thou art,
great and humble,
summoned by one
serene and good
who wilt attend
when all are sat."[5]
Shown his place,
stouthearted Alfred

I 4 finds himself
fitting o'erwhelmed.
Then all a sudden
stops the lyres

4. Humanity, before the gods, is undone. The human being is vulgar and crass compared to that which is eternal. In the Elaean framework, Alfred's response is assumed. H. B. Peters, *Religion*, 27.

5. Is this Flora speaking or perhaps the Grim-Gatekeeper returned? Much has and, I assume, will continue to be written on the subject. For a concise summary of the arguments, see Wilby, *Voices of Sigurd*, 86–112.

and silence fills
the sacred hall.
"Arise assemblage,"
announces the herald,

15 "Jove doth join us
in joyous feast."
Triumphal entry,
towering monarch,
Alfred awes
at Avalonia's king.
Speaking the deep,[6]
sadly Jove laments:

16 "Umbrians broke
boldly with 'laea,
though ever mortal
to o'erthrow the good,
we ascertain
woeful earth little.[7]
Alfred," Jove speaks,
"allow us to ask:

17 "What wrongs have led
to winter's misery?"[8]
King of Elaea,
crowned in Caerpel,
stalwart Alfred
stands to speak:
"Long have we held
loyal and true

---

6. Hardly veiled, this is a clear reference to Psalm 42:7.

7. At least he is honest. Jove here proclaims the gods' aloofness to mortal life.

8. Jove and the gods have taken Elaea's side in Umbria's struggle for statehood. While one can only wonder why, the perspective of both the gods and Alfred will be greatly problematized throughout the poem. Cf. *Sigurd's Lament*, Books X–XII.

18 "to Gramarye's treaty
with great Umbria.[9]
No war shalt be
between bonded states
for tribute in gold
transforms to goods—
ports for trading
and platinum for building.[10]

19 "The boundary fixed
between bonded states,
'tis mirkwooded range—
'tis famed Sherwood.
Neither kingdom can cross
with crude weaponry
or ill intentions
illegally sought.

20 "Egil that Umbrian,
e'en now ruling,
heeded not the tradition
of his noble fathers.[11]
As first snow fell,
foul Egil descended

9. We know very little of this treaty besides what is revealed in the poem and what my father surmises in his "Summary." Much more academic work should and could be done on this point.

10. Though this stanza has been read many ways, most post-colonial theorists find themselves drawn here. What follows would appear to be a description of conquest and oppression from the perspective of the empire. It is both motivated and biased. Who were the Umbrians before the treaty? An enslaved people? A sovereign state conquered in war? Should Alfred and his perspective be believed? Is this section in service to an imperial ideology? What exactly does this section tell us about the poet? While my father ventured his guesses, I will not recount them here, suffice it to say, neither the empire nor their poets are ever what they appear to be. Cf. Ouera, "Life in Oppressive Regimes," 12–27.

11. Egil's transgression is cast as both against the treaty and his forefathers. I wonder how Egil would respond?

'pon the region
proudly negotiated.

2 1 "First felling trees
for war's fearsome toys,
seeking to sabotage
our storied treaty.[12]
Edward I sent,
e'er-true envoy,
who crimson and hewn,
conveying reply,

2 2 "ascended to regions
robbed of life.
His reddened cloak,
received in sorrow,
caused Elaea's king
to cowardly swoon.[13]
Redeeming myself
by rescuing Edward,

2 3 "I bested Anglach
at Grey Gate's battle.
Sorely wounded,
sadly bested,
by poison sickened
purposefully wrought.
A doleful death
demanded payment

2 4 "save the soldier,
the stalwart Edward,
who bound forth
bringing me hither,
forfeiting life

12. "Storied," as in both elegant and accepted.

13. Alfred is so angered by his own response to Edward's death that Alfred refuses to use his own name.

for unfalse friendship.
Unyielding grace,
great god thou art,

25 "have deigned to free
the undone doomed.[14]
Repay I cannot,
poor mortal I am,
but evermore
by service to thee,
I wilt wield crowns
wonderfully light."[15]

26 The speaker startles
as sovereignty laughs—
no malicious intent—
but mirth and merriment.[16]
"In humility
and honor thou thrives,
such that e'en gods
should devoutly study.[17]

27 "Let us feast
in fabled company
and discuss that

14. He is thanking Zeus for forgiving Edward his debt to the gods. Interestingly, Edward is absent from this portion of the banquet.

15. One can only surmise how Alfred wore crowns before. My father wrote: "A king's responsibility is to his country, yes, and to his people, certainly. But above all else, a king's duty is to his soldiers" (*Notes and Letters*, 347). Perhaps this illumines Alfred's statement: "Wonderfully light."

16. How often are the gods happy? Compare with Fitzgerald's elegant translation of Virgil: "Can anger / Black as this prey on the minds of heaven?" (1:18–19).

17. Jove has, before the eyes of the reader, changed. Where once he refused to take note of mortals, he now calls for the gods to study them (V:16, V:26). For more on process theology and open theism in the role of poetry and the novel see, Middleton's corpus: *Novel Theology*; *God, Literature and Process Thought*; *Broken Hallelujah*; and *Theology after Reading*.

deemed aright by nature
apt to our station—
Avalonia's citizens."
A cry went up,
circling the room,

28　as Jupiter sits
in his judgment seat.
The lyres strike
as lavish fare
reveals its worth
to revelers divine.
The fires burning
in fine places

29　create an aura
captivating all.
Alfred succumbs
always joyous—
feasting, singing,
forgetting woe.
A skald then sings,
a singular god,

30　of Anglach's fall,
fashioned in Hel.[18]
The troubadour,
troubled little,
recounts those woes
recently worked.
Alfred sobers,
anguishing much,

18. Already have Alfred's exploits become a thing of myth. "Men act in human ways," my father stated, "the miraculous is rare. It is only later, and not long after, that deeds and actions become that of legend. Once legend, it is only a small step towards religion" (*Notes and Letters*, 235). Cf. Crossan's *Power of Parable* and *Dark Interval*.

3 1 wondering at Edward's
willful absence.
But even in realms
of bright divinity
the day must end,
dark and dreary.
The sun which wheels
wearily in azure,

3 2 rests for mortals
and majesty alike.
Striking, piercing,
the sundering rays
swoop through heaven
surrendering light,
forgetting that
for which they've splayed.

3 3 The beaming fingers
forego their bloom
and gently extinguish
in Jupiter's realm.
The day acquiesces,
darkness now looms,
as Edward erect,
e'er-champion of Elaea,

3 4 enters the feast
filled with doom.
Aglow his eyes,
Alfred heeds,
for e'en gods silence
for spoken prophecy.
Words came next
which revealed history.[19]

---

19. Edward's role has shifted. He is now both seer and prophet. For more
on the many shades of Alfred's cousin, see Alfonso, *Morphed Cousin*, 341–78.

Book VI

Edward, through augury, recounts the foundations of Elaea, the present doom, and that which comes after.

I   "'Twas void of nothing, 'twas verily at peace,"
    Edward the Elder, ever-omen bringer,
    began speaking while surrounded by gods.[1]
    "Neither time nor language
    exists in stasis (though perfected exempla established),[2]
    but neither are begotten nor built.
    From emptiness then, forged and fashioned,
    the Makers created matter and spirit
        and form."[3]
      Enigmatic Edward

1. See the introduction for an explanation on the change in verse and meter.

2. Here is the Platonic concept of forms as put forth by Porphyry. Edward, recounting the Elaean creation myth, claims that "in the beginning" neither time nor language as we know them existed. The Platonic forms for both time and language, however, did. Cf. Plato, *Complete Works*, and Plotinus, *Enneads*.

3. We do not know whom these Elaean Makers were or from whence Edward gleaned his material, but it has much in common with Tolkien's *Silmarillion*. What is of interest here is that these Makers created the matter, spirit, and form that was then used to create the known world. Though similar to Augustine of Hippo (cf. *Confessions* and *City of God*), it is wholly its own in claiming that the Makers made *matter* and that their offspring fashioned reality.

pauses and prepares
his wondrous word-hoard
to dispense crucial cares.

2   "First among gods, great Jüt was figured.
And to him was given the terrible task:
'Carve the world; Create from creation.'[4]
Words thus spoken, were vital to Jüt[5]
who witnessed the speaking wielded by firsts.
Language inaugurated, likewise so time,
with plentiful words wondrous in sum.[6]
Bequeathed in echoes, however, is our bereft speech,
    which desires
    meaning meted by use
    but pales poorly
    when compared with words loosed
by august architects orally.[7]

3   "So sign and referent were sown in synthesis,[8]
and happily Jüt honed his skill—
whole-words worked to weave whole worlds.[9]
Twelve wert spoken and tonally contrived,
but creation's gem, that kingdom of justice,

4. In a way, we are all children of Jüt, running helter-skelter creating our own horrific realities.

5. Much like the Christian myth, Jüt created with words, but in Jüt's case language had already been established.

6. There is no time without language. For to speak is to both proceed and anticipate.

7. In other words, in comparison to Jüt's speech—not to mention the Makers'—our conception of language is infantile.

8. Imagine! Just imagine a world where a word and its referent were one. I, for one, can conceive of no greater paradise. Perhaps that is *Being*. Cf. Wittgenstein, *Philosophical Investigations*; Kristeva, *Desire in Language*; Eco, *Theory of Semiotics*; Eco, *Role of the Reader*; and Eco, *Semiotics and the Philosophy of Language*. For the beginner, I highly suggest Chandler, *Semiotics: The Basics*.

9. "The mind is its own place, and in itself can make a heaven of hell, a hell of heaven," (Milton, *Paradise Lost*, I:254–55).

was last-wrought Elaea both lawful and lush.[10]
In this chosen realm, chancellors wert called:
kings, heroines, and countrymen alike,
      to rightly
   cultivate Elaea's kingdom.
   Long they labored
   weaving with wisdom
   'till equanimity reigned 'tween neighbors.[11]

4 Nothing, however, is natured benign,
but granted choice for good or ill.[12]
Harsh hearths hummed with iron,
as other gods thwarted, grievously so,[13]
Jüt's forged realm, yearning for lordship.
Subtle they were in simulating crafts
that turned men towards unfeigned greed.[14]
Torn asunder, citizens thirsted for
     a day
   when Elaea, elated with peace,
   could sing of sovereign deeds
   done duly to cease
   gnawing, empty fiends.

5 A heroine arose to herald that age.[15]
Regan her name, so regally wrought,
triumphed in glory o'er twelve domains.

10. All in all, Jüt spoke twelve words. Eleven were first spoken, creating eleven kingdoms or worlds. The last word fashioned the apex of creation, Elaea. Mythology is, however, motivated and the other eleven kingdoms are, in their own myths no doubt, the apex of the created order.

11. Waldbergzin, "Odd Couple," 12–56.

12. In the poet's universe, free will reigns supreme.

13. This is obviously in reference to the Elaean-trickster god, Raka. Cf. H. B. Peters, *Distention*, 568.

14. In the Elaean cosmology, greed is the root of all evil, which—it must be stressed—is a human construct both willed and embodied by systems first and then individuals. Cf. H. B. Peters, *Religion*, 423.

15. The recounting of heroes both past and future has much in common with Virgil's *Aeneid* and Milton's *Paradise Lost*.

Long is that song elsewhere sung,
so my passing over it precludes not passion.
Years availed with little aggression
'fore Queen Regan quested and fell.[16]
Sadly her reign surrendered its hold
      by hands
    grotesque. But glory
    she forever found
    in Elaea's stately story,
    'stablishing our royal renown.

6 "Many honest heroes succeeded her
that fabled queen both famous and feared.
Few could compare with her diligent competence,
though numerous tried, uncounted failed.
Ages then passed, jaunting through time,
when realms sorely missed masterly sovereigns.
Kingdoms broke off, creating new states
that drew borders both indelible and fixed.[17]
    Elaeans
    forgot their familiar
    heritage. Hewn and split,
    souls grew superior,
    believing borders such grievances permitted.

7 "Not long after, Alfred arose
to steadily sit on sovereignty's throne.
Much he managed to maneuver quickly,
but surly Umbrians seldom do wait.
This august audience has already heard
of Egil's defiance of Elaea's treaty.
Little more to say of such gross labor,
what I'll speak next is new prophecy
    about
    Elaea's future lionization

16. For more on the life of Queen Regan, see my *Regan*, vol. 4.

17. The nation-state, even in Elaea, was established to the detriment of the world.

where war-forged judgment
and humility's ambition
will overflow like vintage.

8 "Easy to claim difficult to execute,
our once and future, fortuity not controlling,
necessitate Alfred negotiating with sword.
Loose our king languishing in heaven
that we might regain realms once ours.[18]
Nay! Do not intervene most imposing of gods,
before I recount what's really at stake.
Not only acclaim, but also our heroes
    who wilt
      ever employ thy will
      by verily seeking valor
      which by import will instill
      right worship and labor.

9 "First of fabled and future heroes
'tis Finley Goodestroke a fatherless man.[19]
Long wilt he labor with learnéd learning,
in the gilded tower of disguised thaumaturgy.
Well will he win his wonderful knowledge
before uncovering a baleful plot
to untimely undo Elaea's progress.
Finley the boy, finely grown man,
    will reveal
      our country's wrong conceit
      in incorrectly conceiving
      that our realm brings beliefs

18. Once more does Edward implore the powers: Alfred must be loosed or Elaea will be lost. For that which is to come can only transpire if certain actions are taken by Alfred on Elaea's behalf. This would, at first glance, appear to problematize the earlier celebration of Elaean freewill, but in context has less to do with predestination and more to do with the Elaean conception of middle knowledge. Elaeans, it can be said, do not shy away from paradox.

19. For more on Finley Goodestroke, see my *Finley*, vol. 5.

void of vainglory and grief.[20]

I O   "Few will heed Finley's call
      though e'er-established as Elaea's great min'ster.
      Why must we fight when faced with reason
      knowing that nature is nothing if unwieldy?
      More can be mentioned 'bout master Finely,
      but long in lore is that labored story.
      Suffice it to say so skilled will he be
      that Elaea will e'er-recall its enumerable virtues:
            grace,
         honor and humility;
         strength and solidarity;
         gladness, gentility,
         and a principled prosperity.

I I   "Ages will pass parading unceasingly,
      and we will fail Finley's standard.
      Fear not this fall from lofty heights,
      for many a man has madly tumbled.
      The epoch 'tis long 'tween Finley and Nim,
      our next fabled heroine for whom we shall speak.[21]
      Much in that span murderously transpires

20. I am drawing closer. When my father penned "Abe45sxx8" in his marginalia, I first considered it nothing more than a rambling doodle. But, after much reflection, I am beginning to see that perhaps he had stumbled across some kind of ancient cipher. It was, of course, my grandfather who originally found the *Sigurd* manuscript, but was without the necessary recourse to translate it. After dying, he passed the manuscript on to my father who was able to translate it, but was unable to complete the full manuscript before passing away himself. He left it to me to complete his academic work on *Sigurd's Lament*. What I am beginning to see, however, is that my grandfather found more than one document that day, but only revealed the *one* to my father, who in turn only revealed *Sigurd* to me. My father must have, through some unknown avenue, discovered this and gone in search of Basil's other findings—for who can say, perhaps there are many texts locked away in some old attic, even now structuring our thoughts. I am far from unearthing the full truth, but I can see now that the "Abe" in "Abe45sxx8" is the abbreviation of my father's childhood home: Aberdylwyth. Perhaps it is time for my return.

21. For more on Nim, see my *Greer*, vol. 6-II.

bringing Elaea to its lamentable brink.
>Destruction
>and woe are wickedly wrought
>before bravery can find
>a clear space to sprout
>and pollinate a paragon's mind.

I 2 "Nim the nameless, now arising,
finds herself hesitant and weary.
The Downfall destroyed, in ruinous manner,
all reality rightly remembered.
Society skewed 'tween Established
and Albalonga, awake will Nim
Elaea's long dormant and slumbering boldness.
Failing at first 'fore finding her way
>Nim must
>begin with regaining
>what once was woefully lost.
>Shrugging off her shame,
>she keenly cedes the cost.

I 3 "Toiling towards this grim-gotten target,
Nim will be harried horribly by her foes.
Long will she rot and languish in prison
'fore freeing herself and fate's hero, Dardan.[22]
Their life reset, resembling birth,
they wilt together establish a novel Elaea.
Wanton tragedy will turn to hope,
as Nim the nameless is nameless no longer.
>'Hope,'
>a silly word seldom
>forgotten, but few
>can avoid life's venom,
>which eagerly eschews.[23]

---

22. The allusion to the Trojans cannot be missed.

23. The poet here reveals his grim outlook on life. For him, life will slowly poison its victims. For more, see Cumbrinar, *Life of the Assassin*, 345.

14 "Surely and sadly, all seasons pass
with the rising and setting of infinite suns.
Long Elaea gloried in its gifted leaders,
but surly gods have sanctified memories.
The Destroyer, dank and deceitful,
will at the last return to wreak his ruin.
Why will we, we good people,
forgo what is good for small gratifications?[24]
    Mystery,
    or rather, mysteries
    proliferate plentifully,
    when hammered by history
    we fail to be faithful.

15 "This then 'tis thoroughly inescapable,
for fate has decreed that worlds shall fail:
Time will come to close together with discourse
when woeful beasts, though wonderfully beheld,
escape Hel and invade Elaea.[25]
The Deceiver controlling these doomed creatures,
war will rage wearing sturdy warriors.
Kingdoms shall burn, crumbling in ruin,
    Forever
    destroyed. Woe and death
    shall surely reign
    banishing weakened breaths
    provoking dismal pains.

16 "From what far corner shall faith be kept?
To where shall aid, wretchedly needed,
be fast bound and bountifully found?
In a word, we few, we now
will establish this hope that will win Elaea.

24. "Why will we, we good people, / forgo what is good for small gratifications?" If ever this poem reaches to greater heights, then it is most certainly here.

25. According to Edward, the Elaean Ragnarök is the collapsing of time and language. Cf. H. B. Peters, *Religion*, 23.

'Nay!' You note, both knowledgeable and wise,
'How canst the future
be controlled from the present?'"[26]
At this Edward paused,
preparing his prophecy.
      Glowing
    eyes with stern words
    tumbled forth terribly.
    Few could blur
    Edward's visioned verity.

I 7   "The future is fairly forgotten by gods
for immortality knows nothing of change.[27]
But we, we mortals, from moment to moment,
live in lucid reality. Lore is long
that speaks of battles and that serious sundering,
which 'tis a myth made myth no longer:[28]
gods must generously free a great and good king,
though bound in heaven, bound for battle.
      Alfred,
    to precipitate proud victory
    in that final fray,
    must be loosed from heaven's history
    and travel to death's day."[29]

26. Indeed.

27. For an exploration into changelessness and divinity, see Uppsalla, *Eternal Stasis*, 23–56.

28. What would happen—seriously—what would happen if our myths came true?

29. It is confirmed: Alfred must die.

Book VII

Jupiter relents and releases Alfred to his fate, the king bids Edward farewell, and Alfred, ending his time in Avalonia, descends to Elaea.[1]

I   Edward the Elder,
    ever-champion of Elaea,
    crisply closes
    his consequential prophecy.
    Silence reigns and
    rolls through the hall
    as great gods
    gloomily cogitate.

2   Much was mentioned
    with meaningful words
    that though long days
    to think and reflect,

1. As already has been mentioned, the arguments of each book were later scribal additions (or so my father thought) and here it is interesting that Jüt or Zeus is now called by his Roman name, Jupiter. It is as if the poet first and the scribe second were interested in collapsing the whole of the mythological tradition into this one poem. In doing so, the effect is equal parts distention's bloom and Oulipo's anticipatory plagiarism. One cannot help but wonder, however, that if myth can be employed in such a manner in text, then how can it be utilized in practice? Cf. the introduction above, and Bayard, "Anticipatory Plagiarism."

still there be
time too little.
Deities, like mortals,
must discharge destined duties.[2]

3 Into silence,
serene and sturdy,
Jupiter speaks judiciously
with these just words:
"Hope is nothing
'less honorably gained,
and though we deem
thy deeds important,

4 "we would still wish
thou waited here.
But the last battle
is bearing towards us
and prophecy
properly tells us
that away to Avalonia
Alfred must go.[3]

5 Though great I am
in grace and wisdom,
if death shall bring
the Deceiver to account,
than doomed thou be,
for die thou must."[4]
Jupiter pauses,
the just and high,

6 turns towards Alfred

2. Time will, even for gods, beat unceasingly.

3. For more on Jupiter's acquiescence to prophecy, see H. B. Peters, *Religion*, 252.

4. Alfred, in a harsh twist, becomes the cosmos' tool to affect (among many) one of its predetermined paths.

and talks once more:
"Who am I—
wonderful to behold—
to raze fate or
ruin time?
'Jupiter,' you say,
'the joyous god,'

7 "but what's a name
that wants in power?[5]
Even I, a deity,
must e'er deign to stars.[6]
Though I see before me
a bright king and
a proud man,
pityingly I acquiesce
            to predestined prophecy.

8 "King of Elaea,
kind-hearted Alfred,
from 'Ionia thou
must leave at last.
Banished thou art not,
but bravely asked:
Will thou prepare
providence's way?"[7]

---

5. Again, we see the poet lamenting the harsh disconnection between a word and its referent. As long as this divide exists, he seems to be saying, no god—let alone a mortal—can find that for which he or she longs. In the end, the chasm between language and experience results in the hopeless enduring of fate's whim.

6. In no mythological corpus is Jupiter considered a "joyous" god. The poet here is taking great liberties to present an Elaean version of Jüt, Zeus, Jupiter, or Jove that is categorically different from that of tradition. Though Boileau would, no doubt, find much wanting in the poet's depiction of Jupiter, we must remember that this is a Jupiter for Elaea, not a Jove for Italy. Cf. Boileau-Despréaux, "Art of Poetry," 241–52.

7. And yet! And yet, Alfred is given a choice. Fate binds all; choose freely. The paradox is overwhelming to my Western sensibilities. Where is this Elaea

9 Alfred stands
astute and stern:
"Long have I rested
near 'Ionia's hearth,
but battles ne'er wait
for befitting times.
I will go
and gorge on blood,[8]

IO "for kings cannot
comfortably abstain.
That Umbrian,
the unfortunate soul,
will find fate
fickle and cruel."[9]
Raising his glass
with resounding woe,

II Alfred toasts
in agony plain.
Few believe
his boastful words
recognizing fear
and resigning fate.
Rather than weep
with royal dolor,

I2 the august audience
answers the king

that I might *choose* to live?

8. And here we see war depicted in its cruel glory. While rooting for Alfred and wanting to see him triumph, we will watch him become a kind of grotesque anti-hero, a warrior who feasts on blood. For more on this, see Dickson, *Blood of the Guilty*, 398–434.

9. Alfred desires fate to be kind to him, but fickle to his enemy. Eco's *Prague Cemetery* and *Inventing the Enemy* are wonderful explorations into the necessity of an enemy for the shaping of ones identity.

with solemn dignity
suitable for heroes.
Fair Flora stands,
fitted with elegance:
"Arise ye hosts,
and to Alfred bow,

I 3 "for here mere mortals
illuminate gods.[10]
Where we would fail,
wearily he goes
to fight our battle,
to fell our enemy."
Swiftly sweeping
through sovereign chambers

I 4 loud laudations
from loyal hands
arise for Alfred
from Avalonia's hosts.
Weeping he bows,
bending to weird,[11]
knowing the honor
now bestowed

I 5 by gracious gods
goes rarely forth.[12]
Rising with reticence,
he recalls Edward,
and turns to true friend
posed to talk:
"Edward, ever-kindred,
to Elaea I go.

---

10. What a wonderful idea! Perhaps we mortals shape the gods in our image? For more on this, see Durkheim, *Elementary Forms of Religious Life*.

11. "Weird" or "fate" or "destiny" or "doom."

12. The gods are rather stingy with their praise.

16 "Sadness finds me
sundered from you.
Long have we ranged,
lingering little,
performing deeds
proudly done.
Brothers together,
we braved the world,

17 "few could tame us
few would try.
Mastering Elaea
as men and kings
we found such joy
flowing from life.[13]
E'en death victorious
met with disaster.

18 "To Anglach's pit
I proudly journeyed
to wrest my brother
from wretched fire.
Quickly we conquered
that careening demon
and embraced our fate
on 'Ionia's fringe.

19 "Our darkest hour
I deem that night,
but even then
we fiercely battled."
Alfred, pauses,
awe inspiring,

13. Much has been written on this and the following speech. Perhaps
Alfred and Edward did have a romantic relationship with one another and
perhaps they were just two old warriors. Who can say? But if this sort of thing
interests you, look no further: Warmhurst, *Sex in Sigurd*, 68–90, and Lee,
Hamlet Sheared, 132–39.

and embraces Edward,
Elaea's champion.

20 "Enough has been said,
numerous times recounted.
I must away
and mourn no longer.
Come what will,
crippled or killed,
I will win my way
through worlds to you."[14]

21 Edward bows
burying his face
to hide his tears
hurrying down.
For mournful wars
though maddened and mean
birth bonds
barely understood.[15]

22 Greatly grieves
that grave warrior
before bracing
brother and king.
"Lo! I lingered
long in Hel
with wounds and worry
for weary companions.

23 "Then thou came,
thy king and cousin,
to split that fiend

14. I need not tell you, dear reader, that this line was hurled to stardom by the now famous blockbuster-movie series *Through Worlds to You*, directed by I. O. Craften.

15. For a vigorous defense of Alfred and Edward's relationship, see Ajani, "Warmhurst Is Wrong," 113–56.

from his spirit.
I cannot repay
such a royal deed,
not with words
that woefully fail.

24 "So when thou seest
that surly Umbrian,
wield my sword
wonderfully blessed."
Edward now pulls
by pommel his blade
from out his scabbard
scribbled with runes.[16]

25 "Forged from fire
fit for kings,
this blade bestows
upon its bearer
the advised ability
to ascertain aright
runes and charms
etched 'pon thine enemies."[17]

26 With these words,
Edward weeping,
hands his sword,
the Harbinger,[18]

16. It is passing strange that Dardan is here forgotten. Alfred is, in Dardan's absence, given Edward's sword to combat Egil. He will also soon be given a gift from Flora. More will be said upon the matter in a later footnote.

17. Here is another strange reference. Edward seems to think that Egil will have magicians in his employ, magicians who will dress him in all manner of runes and lorecraft. Edward's sword, however, has the power to expose Egil's magical trifles. This is, of course, superfluous, for as the reader will soon discover, upon Alfred's return to Elaea, all references to magic or magical items are thoroughly excoriated from the poem. Neither this sword nor Egil's runes will ever again be seen.

18. "Harbinger." Cf. Fuligin, *Terminus Est*, 25–78.

to king and cousin,
the courageous Alfred.
"Forgo thy woes,"
fair Flora says,

27 "And weep little more
when Alfred wends.
Time will reveal
how royalty fares.
Now from Avalonia
must Alfred go,
but I will depart
to assist his descent."

28 Taking her hand
with hopeful heart,
Alfred follows Flora
to 'Ionia's fringe.[19]
Bathed in light
beaming through clouds,
Flora stops
and sternly speaks:

29 "Much has moved
meandering heaven,
but rarely doth we,
we royal gods,
agree with the accord
issued to Alfred.[20]
Take heart in time
teaming with thee."

30 Flora then falters,
fearing her speech:
"Last words linger
long on our minds,

19. Once more Alfred stands at the edge of heaven.
20. Flora admits that the gods rarely agree upon history's direction.

for how should we speak
such sudden doom?"
Alfred answers:
"Anon I go,

31 "so swiftly say."
Sadly Flora utters:
"'Ionia's light
lingers little
and soon will surrender
it's strength and aura.
What the Umbrian,
ungainly and false,

32 "has brought to bear
'tis burdensome for all.
If victorious
o'er vanquished enemy,
'Ionia will sunder,
but no longer shrivel.[21]
'Tis not your trouble
to navigate treachery

33 "reaped in heaven
by reputed gods.
Dim we must,
dim we shall,
but light from 'Ionia
will lead thy way.
Take this cloak,
and clad thyself,

34 for sown in seams

21. Flora reveals to Alfred that with the Umbrian's actions, Avalonia's light
is dimming. Alfred's actions could stem the tide, but only so far as to keep the
light from extinguishing. Even if Alfred is successful, the realm of the gods will
forever be sundered from Elaea. This is a common theme in mythopoeic litera-
ture and it is not surprising to find it here. For more, see Tolkien's *Silmarillion*;
History of Middle Earth; and *Tree and Leaf: Including Mythopoeia*.

is sovereign light.
Last though it be,
lustrous it is.
Wield it well
'gainst weary foes."[22]
Alfred then bowed,
awed by Avalonia.

22. After receiving a sword from Edward, Alfred is now awarded a golden cloak from Flora. In it, she claims that the very light of heaven is weaved. For our purposes, much has been posited on these objects, but it is now generally agreed upon that these are the long lost and fabled rewards that Beowulf received from King Hrothgar after slaying Grendal's mother. Cf. Heaney, *Beowulf*, 915–1231, and Lima, "Lost Gifts of Beowulf," 34–89.

Book VIII

Alfred descends through snow and fire, finds a winter-weary Elaea longing for the stirrings of spring, and then rises to rouse his warriors.

I With sword and cloak,
swiftly Alfred steps
o'er golden paths,
'neath gleaming gateways,
bowing his bright head
before doomed fate.
Turning his gaze
towards the clouds,

2 he claims farewell
'fore fair Flora.
With one step,
sliding forward,
Alfred awakens
to Elaea's allurement.
His body begins
to burgeon with life,

3 but not before—
his breath escapes—
snowcapped crests,

coursing waters,
jutting pines and
joyous fauna—
kind-hearted Alfred,
Elaea's king,

4 returns to gravity
groaning his name.[1]
When seething snow
starts its descent,
does Alfred ascend
to acquire his doom.[2]
Soft and serene,
slow and sturdy,

5 does winter's grip
grab hold of warriors.
Fear falls then
and forges cowards,
who wearily wait
for winter's end.
While war does work
its woeful ends,

6 the frozen field
forged in blood
lays long dormant

---

1. The land is intimately linked with Elaea's true king. Here we see creation groaning at Alfred's return. My grandfather, Basil, who was Welsh, once said to my father (or so said my father, Wallace, for I never met my grandfather): "The empire will write whatever it likes to prop up its stupidest subjects—the king being most heavily fortified."

2. The poet takes us back to Alfred's ascension at winter's first snow and the decision to "wait it out" until spring. In lines 7–10, however, the poet calls this a decision of "cowards." Throughout the poem, we have been led to believe that the poet is against armed conflict, but perhaps the situation is not so clear. The poet's position on warfare and the enemy will only become more and more problematized as the poem progresses.

as liminal space.[3]
Between bold armies
burdened with snow,
no battles rage
and no blood spills.

7 Patient and proud
do Paladins wait
for kind-hearted Alfred,
famed king of Elaea,
to die a death
designated weak.[4]
Few of his followers
hold fast to hope.

8 Alfred's young Captain,
Crispin so called,
gathers his generals
'neath great oak[5]
as winter's weariness
begins to weaken:
"Our Lord t'was lost,
low-brought by treachery.

9 "Little labor we did
languishing through Yule,[6]
but now we need
to navigate a course.

3. Where a forest once separated these two kingdoms, there is now only a field.

4. The Elaeans in Alfred's camp are certain of Alfred's death and are now waiting for him to pass so that they can make their final decision. For more, see Tremolo, "Cowards in Winter," 34–189.

5. This is Crispin's third gathering beneath the oak. My father vehemently disagreed with me, but I believe this to be a clear allusion to Saint Peter.

6. Yule is the longest day of the Elaean winter and as such a holiday of great import. It is said that Elaeans of all stripes descend upon the castle for a banquet thrown by the king or queen. Much has been written on this egalitarian day of festivities, but for a full recounting of one such holiday, see my *Regan*.

The task 'fore us:
triumph in war
or wait wondering
for wounded King?"

10 From out the *comitatus*,[7]
calls forth a voice,
a rough-hewn ranger,
who rules men well:
"We will wait no longer
as weary men,
for sun and spring
are sure to come.

11 "Act we must
on Alfred's behalf,
'fore the false Umbrian
finds us unprepared."
Many men agree
with tactical Marius,[8]
the rough-hewn ranger,
who reasons well.

12 Crispin then, clearheaded,
clashes sword and shield.
"As the dawn doth crawl,
does death draw nigh.[9]
Let the lame Egil
linger in bed
as we few,
we weary warriors,

---

7. A Latin word meaning "company" or "armed group."

8. Marius is a man for action. He is ready to put Alfred to rest and war with the Umbrian. Marius, of course, if not a factual figure, then most certainly is a character ripped from Victor Hugo's most wonderful of works, *Les Misérables*.

9. The full renunciation. Cf. Quenya, *When the Cock Crows*, 34–78.

I 3   "seek sad vengeance
for sundered kings.
Five will find
the falsifiers in camp
and bleed them badly
before they wake.
With cries and clanging,
our controlled army

I 4   will then work woe
on Wōden's enemies.[10]
Should any shutter
'fore such shedding,
then speak thy words
throwing thyself on mercy."[11]
All is silent,
serene, and still

I 5   as clear-eyed Crispin
combs the crowd.
"Then it is done.
Thanes: thrice prepare,
for meek men
will offer mercy
when tears of terror
trickle from enemies.

I 6   "Tomorrow, we cannot
tangle our hearts
with such naïve
and softhearted sympathy."[12]

---

10. And here is a new name for the Elaean god at the top of the Elaean pantheon. We can only wonder if Elaean's actually had five names for Jüt or if the poet is taking license for the purpose of alliteration.

11. Alfred's army will seek to slaughter their enemies while they sleep. Crispin asks for those who cannot stomach such a task to admit it and stay abed. But no one, not a one, speaks out.

12. Crispin admits that killing a warrior in his or her sleep is a brutal affair

Erect and awful,
astute Crispin
turns towards 'Ionia
and thanks true gods.[13]

17 Then, as the first
thick snowfall[14]
starts with slow,
small flakes
and, given time,
grows into a gale,
or a fire flickers
into fleeting life

18 before brightly burning
with bold brilliance,
a whispered name
whirls through camp.
Man turns to man
masking hopes
long lying dormant
in lingering winter.

19 "Alfred," she says,[15]
shuttling back and forth,
between weary warriors
boldly preparing.
Crispin, clear-headed,
turns and calls:
"Who whispers to men
when wholly invisible?

that most people are likely to balk at, but his answer is hard and clear. As my
father used to say: "Steel the soul to whet the blade."

13. For a thoughtful exploration into religion and violence in the middle
ages, cf. Kaeuper, *Chivalry and Violence* and *Holy Warriors.*

14. Petit, *Snows of Sigurd*, 167: "When snow falls in *Sigurd's Lament,*
something is about to happen. Pay attention!"

15. Who is whispering? Flora?

20 "Who awakens in men
   a dead warmth?"
   Answers the rhetor:
   "Alfred. Alfred."
   No longer confused,
   Crispin cries out:
   "To the tent!
   To the king's tent!"[16]

21 Marching madly
   with tactical Marius,
   Crispin catapults,
   careening, heedless,
   into the tent
   of his true lord.
   Eyes adjusting
   in the ever-dim,

22 Crispin catches sight,
   confused, astonished,
   of risen Alfred,
   resurrected from death.[17]
   Numb and kneeling,
   he unknots his brow.
   "Long-laying Lord,"
   he lowly whispers,

23 "hearts hurdle despair
   hearing of thy rise.
   'Tis true, my Lord,
   that thou hast returned?"
   Alfred, awe inspiring,
   acknowledges none,
   but speaks in secret

16. Crispin's denial is soon overcome.

17. The theme of resurrection in literature is well known and hardly deserves a footnote.

with hidden susurrations.[18]

24 "What words are those
my weary lord speaks?
Who is Flora?
What 'forever debt?'"
Alfred then answers,
articulate and strong,
"Crispin, my captain,
I call on thee now:

25 "gather grim men,
Elaea's great warriors,
for forthright kings
must admit their folly.
All will be answered,
all will be given.
Now collect my knights
near the bleak oak."[19]

26 Crispin strides to camp,
crying gaily;
Marius marches
matching shouts;
weary and war torn
warriors bend their ears—
"The king, the king,"
the exclamations say,

27 "Hast happily returned
to herald victory.
Quick now, quick now,
congregate 'neath the oak,

18. We can only ask: "What was Jesus, with his dark finger, drawing in the sand?" Likewise, we can only ask: "What was Alfred, freshly awakened, whispering with hidden words?" Cf. John 8:6.

19. And so we return to the tree! This is the fourth and final time. A return to the scene of Crispin's denial.

for the king's speech
can stall no longer."
Up they arise,
answering their captains

28 with swift-footed actions
and ferocious shouts.
Moving, stumbling,
men sweep forward,
fumbling towards fate
with folly's ignorance.
"There!" they shout,
"there's our high thane."

29 And beneath the oak
but before his men,
the paramount stands,
preeminent among fighters.
A hush falls fully
on that fearful crowd,
seeing their sovereign
after long spans.

30 "Avalonia," Alfred speaks,[20]
"is filled with awe—
not that of mortal men,

20. The poet fails where Shakespeare succeeds (*Henry V*, IV:18–67): "This day is call'd the feast of Crispian. / He that outlives this day, and comes safe home, / Will stand a tip-toe when this day is nam'd, / And rouse him at the name of Crispian. / He that shall live this day, and see old age, / Will yearly on the vigil feast his neighbours, / And say 'To-morrow is Saint Crispian.' / Then will he strip his sleeve and show his scars, / And say / These wounds I had on Crispian's day.' / Old men forget; yet all shall be forgot, / But he'll remember, with advantages, / What feats he did that day ... / And Crispin Crispian shall ne'er go by, / From this day to the ending of the world, / But we in it shall be remembered— / We few, we happy few, we band of brothers; / For he to-day that sheds his blood with me / Shall be my brother; be he ne'er so vile, / This day shall gentle his condition; / And gentlemen in England now-a-bed / Shall think themselves accurs'd they were not here, / And hold their manhoods cheap whiles any speaks / That fought with us upon Saint Crispin's day."

but that of immortal gods.
I have been.
I have seen.
Rolling hills
regal in splendor,

3 1 "golden halls
glistening with aura.
But so too the bane,
that baleful beast
that malevolent Anglach,
miserable to the end.
So I have spied gods
and seen splendors,

3 2 "and all has pointed,
acute and piercing,
to this moment,
to this time.
Yes, I yielded,
for yesterday's memory
was built with burdens
bearing Edwardian woes.[21]

3 3 "But lying in 'Ionia,
lucid dialogue I had
with wondrous Edward,
e'er warrior of Elaea.
He told me tales
with tremendous meaning
of Elaea's past and present
and prophetic future.

3 4 "Long I lingered
lying abed,
but now I stand

21. The king here admits that his swoon at the death of Edward was a
cowardly act.

with supernal sparks.
Fate no longer faceless
falls before us
with wide arms
waiting for grim-warriors
        to wrest their destiny."[22]

22. *Sigurd's Lament* rarely reaches the peaks of those poems with which it is in direct lineage. But there are moments, lines here and there, that do say something capable of moving the reader. This is one such place: "Fate no longer faceless / falls before us / with wide arms / waiting for grim-warriors / to wrest their destiny." My father—having returned from WWI, remember—would often quote this to himself in moments of great stress. Sadly, those moments were often instigated by either my mother, Eined, or me. My mother was Welsh through and through and had no intentions of marrying a translator, a man of letters and education. Hers was a long tradition of able-bodied shepherds. But the man she fell in love with before the war, she once confided in me, was *not* the man who returned. There were moments, sad moments, of both abuse and scandal. I once asked Eined why she never left Wallace, but she would not say. That was, in fact, why I left and promised never to return. It was not until years later that I did. My father was on his death bed. I went home to say goodbye. And for his last act, he pulled me into his world, the world of *Sigurd's Lament*.

Book IX

Alfred dons his armor before treating with Egil on a melting battlefield surrounded by the jostling hosts of insatiable warriors.

1　After arousing men,
　　Alfred retreats to tent
　　and begins to don
　　his burdensome armor.
　　Spying his silvered
　　and sturdy panoply,
　　he stoops to strap
　　and secure his fit.

2　And what worried words
　　can we wearily say
　　about the thinking thane
　　that readies for war?
　　Death deals blows
　　to determined minds
　　and weak willed warriors
　　without prejudice.

3　Alfred, ever astute,
　　acknowledges his heart
　　beating within his breast

at breakneck speeds.
Is it fear that fastens
to his fierce mind
or the unknown knowledge
of his knightly enemy?

4 But wait, we say,
with warranted confusion,
does not this doom-bringer
know his destiny,
has he not hastened
to heaven's door?
Be neither keen nor quick
to stand in court

5 and preemptively pronounce
a pitiable judgment
upon the proud warrior
who precedes to war.
We, we in comfort,
are without the burdens
brought on by slaughter
that surface from blood.

6 We who will labor
and work for bread,
know not the knight
who kills in kind.
Weep we may
for woeful warrior,
but to question and query
is cancerous indeed.[1]

---

1. Here the voice of the poet breaks through both verse and meter to make itself known. He asks us why humanity so readily judges the motivations of the warrior. For who is the baker or the banker or the bailiff to question the man or woman of warfare? As Benjamin John Peters in *Through All the Plain* has so aptly shown, the warrior is a complex signification in any culture. Plato called the warrior to philosophy and concern for the city, Sun Tzu to patience and grace, and the Christian God to peace and justice. Oh, certainly, adherents

7   Now fitted for fighting,
    the fabled king assembles
    his captains and knights,
    his doomed countrymen.
    Arrayed in armor
    awesome to behold,
    Alfred's army
    arrives at the field.[2]

8   Across from Alfred
    at the Mirkwood's hem
    in another camp
    arising at dawn,
    gruff Egil gathers,
    guessing at fate,
    his adroit advisors
    to await their advice.[3]

9   The baleful Umbrian,
    burdened with weight,
    speaks with strain,
    but singular clarity:
    "Long have we labored
    under liege-lords,

to these various philosophies have lived out different codes of violence widely careening away from the gravitational orbs of their founders, but in his or her idealized state the warrior has always signified fidelity, sacrifice, and—in a strange, sick way—hope. War is humankind's grasping of fate in its own two hands and hurling death back at the gods. And yet, the poet knows—has acknowledged even—that war is a desperate and bloody affair manipulated by both the state and its mythologies. No, it is not beautiful. No, it is not elegant. But it provides us, as does all loss, a rare glimpse into our own humanity. Without it, how would we become that which we are? Without war, the poet asks us to consider, what is art?

   2. For more on the themes of war and the warrior in *Sigurd's Lament*, see Marin, "Lords of War and Play," 98–143, and Trandy, "Violence Is a Sick Purple," 231–56.

   3. Having loomed large over the narrative, we now get a second, in-depth view into Egil's camp.

oppressed and persecuted
by a privileged few.[4]

10   "But why? I beg.
Because they think them better.
Do I not bleed
when brought low by blades?
Does my mind not mutate
when mastered overlong?
Do I not dream and desire
for a dutiful life?[5]

11   "Does my war-weary wife
warrant less than Alfred's?[6]
No. But treated as naught
because naught—
as a muddled image
in a dusty mirror—
is the sight we see
when spying ourselves.[7]

12   "The time has transpired
to challenge those tyrants

4. In one stanza, all that we thought we knew about *Sigurd's Lament* is turned on its head. No longer is Alfred the hero working his way through fate towards a great evil manifested in Egil. Alfred, rather, is an oppressive liege lord and master ruling from his throne in far away Caerpel. Perhaps all along what we have heard is propaganda funded by the Elaean state? Perhaps the poet tired of his role as courtier and decided to wield his creative powers to undo the structures of systemic violence and injustice? Perhaps we will never know and the poet here is asking us to see something new in our enemies— their humanity? Cf. Geoffrey, *Propaganda as a Poetic Device*, 314.

5. Cf. Fanon, *Black Skin, White Masks* and *The Wretched of the Earth*.

6. This is a moment of shear vulnerability on Egil's part. We learn that not only is Egil married, but so also is Alfred. And what a question: "Does my war-weary wife / warrant less than Alfred's?" *Of course not!* the reader wants to bellow, before catching him- or herself and realizing that Egil is the enemy and an enemy's wife deserves nothing. See Mandry, "Wives and Their Authors," 156–78.

7. Cf. Lacan, *Écrits*, 75–81.

who would work our ruin
while wickedly stealing
our life, our land
and our right labor."[8]
Here he paused,
preparing his words.

I 3   "Below in battle
brave enemies array.
I see them now,
no longer negligent.
Alfred has arisen,
awoken to life,
to lead his land force
as an alarming general.

I 4   "So weigh in now
on our weird and doom:
Should we surrender
our sovereign claim
to forge as free men
our final path
or should we brutally strive
to shuck off brutal kings?"[9]

I 5   Silence fills the space,
serene and heavy,
as Egil, ever-warrior,
eyes his advisors.
Magnus, a man feared,
a master architect,
speaks solemnly,
starting and finishing

I 6   the conversation
the counselors conduct.

8. Alfred has not been such a good king.
9. Egil, never wordy, gives his version of the Saint Crispin's Day Speech.

"We fully follow thee,
not for fate's sake,
but for thine faithfulness
to freedom's ideal.[10]
To an Umbrian man,
we make thee master.

17 "Now, Lord, lead us
to long-labor in battle."
Grim Egil nods,
before gravely kneeling
and speaking words
that resound through history:[11]
"Proud and noble people
serve not their paramount,

18 "but rather their paramount
proudly serves his people."
Rising now as royalty,
readying his warriors,
the brave, grand Egil
gathers his strength
and rides forth
to the field of rest.

19 Two terrible armies,
terrible to behold,
are serenely sundered
by a vast, green surface.
Between the battle-ready
lies a bold pasture

10. Whereas Alfred would claim the divine right to rule, Egil and his advisors claim no such right. For Egil, both his right to rule and lead in battle come from his commitment to the ideal of freedom from oppression. The poet impresses upon the reader that should Egil sway from this commitment then would the Umbrians choose a new leader.

11. See my *Regan*, *Finley*, and *Greer* stories for how Egil's words echoed throughout history, both past and future.

purging winter
to prepare for spring.

2 0 There in the middle,
the thicket of Kore,[12]
blooms a bulb
betokening hope.
The Elaean Crocus,
Winter's Bane, so called,
for its blue bloom
is winter's blue death.[13]

2 1 The vanguard though valiant
verily treads
'pon that vast field
e'er proclaiming promise.
Two men meet
in the middle of armies,
ready to treat
with their royal partner.

2 2 "Alfred," says Egil,
acknowledging his adversary,
"Hardy in health
thou heartily seems,
perhaps mine spies,
planted in thy party
lied to liege lords
'bout thee lingering abed?"

2 3 "Nay," the knight says,
"night had certainly descended,

12. Neither me nor my father could unearth the meaning of the phrase,
"The thicket of Kore." Though many have tried to define Kore, little progress
has been made. Hugh Y. Vertincort has posited an interesting theory, but it is
most certainly phantasmagorical and not worth the reader's time.

13. See Hunt, *Crocus*, 158, and Mabeuf, *Flora of the Environs of Cauteretz*,
34.

but awakened I am
and feeling alive."
Breaking all form,
Alfred bandies:
"Spies you say,
slinking in camps?"

24 Egil, e'er grim,
grins indeed.
"What are secrets
when surrounded by armies?
One will live
and one will die,
but I think not
that both shall thrive."[14]

25 "Yea," says Alfred,
"your thoughts do echo
the alarming words
active in mine mind."
Pausing before parceling
his precise thoughts,
Alfred acknowledges
his awesome foe.

26 Arrayed in grey armor,
with axe and sword,
Egil towers o'er Alfred
and gains much in reach.[15]
With beard and brow,
both burdened with age,
Alfred speaks next
with awful regret.[16]

---

14. They are both aware of their own fates.

15. It is interesting, as I have already pointed out, that no mention is made of either Alfred's well-won rewards or Egil's thaumaturgical runes.

16. I have returned. I am in Aberdylwyth, which I identified as the abbreviation "A–b–e" found in "Abe45sxx8." This is my childhood home, the one

27 "Why would kings
when faced with conflict
make orphans of many
when the many we serve?[17]
Can not you and I,
as kings of old,
settle this strife
in single combat?"

28 Egil, no orator,
but great in honor,
speaks true sentences,
cementing his fame.
"Aye, king Alfred,
I accept thy claim
to invoke *holmgang*
with thy humble enemy.[18]

29 "But let it be said
by few and by many
that e'er grim Egil,
for the good of all,
would kneel before kings,
true knight to true knight,
before irrevocably battling
Umbria's bane."[19]

---

from which I ran so quickly. My father was terrible to me here. His drinking
. . . well, I am here nonetheless. After making a thorough search of the prop-
erty, I located a scratched floorboard in the attic. In an old script etched with
what must have been a knife, I read: "4–5–s." What it means, I cannot be sure,
but I have with me both crowbar and pliers. I will soon peal the board back
and reveal what my grandfather really found that day so long ago in the Welsh
countryside. Wish me luck. Perhaps what was broken can once more be—wait
. . . what was that noise? Did you hear—

17. Both the poet and the kings know something of warfare.

18. "Holmgang" is a duel between two parties to settle disputes.

19. On the battlefield there is neither king nor ruler, but only the knight,
a man of eminent honor. There are many, no doubt, who would take issue with

30 Having spoken hard words,
    Herculean Egil dismounts
    and bows his head
    to blameless Alfred.
    "Kings we art,"
    Elaea's crowned speaks,
    "caught by our countries
    in candied webs.

31 "Wert all weary foes
    as worthy as you,
    perhaps principled kingdoms
    could parley with hope."
    "If wishing were so,"
    the warrior responds,
    "then our royal reigns
    would not rent us so.

32 "But bountifully burdened
    with bitter realities,
    I could no more treat
    than thou could o'er turn
    centuries of slavery."[20]

this depiction of warfare and the honorable knight, who would pose questions of oppression, injustice, and poverty—but what can be said in response? We sometimes do that which we know is stupid, but has been reinforced by countless myths. Cf. White: "But it was too late for another effort . . . For that time it was his destiny to die . . . The fate of this man or that man was less than a drop, although it was a sparkling one, in the great blue motion of the sunlit sea. The cannons of his adversary were thundering in the tattered morning when the Majesty of England drew himself up to meet the future with a peaceful heart" (*Once and Future King*, 639).

20. Ah! And here it is. While the men as men revere one another, there is very little that either can do. They are history's fools, cast to and fro. Alfred inherited a system of injustice and it fell to Egil to challenge the very same. Alfred was an owner; Egil his slave. And who points the finger? We are all implicated in the structures of death, and death, eventually, must come to all. Cf. Munroe, *Ides of Sigurd*, 78–99, and Bumburry, "Slaves We Once Owned," 43–86.

Standing Egil mounts,
turns his warhorse,
and trots towards fate.

33 Warriors returned,
worn down by war,
to predestined camps
preparing for combat:
awe-inspiring Alfred,
always vigilant
and grim-hearted Egil,
e'er genuine.

34 Caught in the cacophony
of cruel history,
propelled forward
by privileged men,
our warriors waking
with wondrous suns
would arise to aurora
radiantly ablaze.[21]

21. For the blending of Aurora with hope, fate, and tragedy, see Gamgee, *With the Sun We'll Rise Only to Die*, 781–82.

Book X[1]

In which death casts its silky web and Sigurd,[2] Egil's son, enters the story.

I Dawn dooms the strong
and downcast alike.
Would that we could wend
our way through fate
and find a fitting direction
for our fabled lives,
but both tales and truth
have this in common:

1. The poet's voice and the poem's perspective shifts so drastically in the last three books that there are new academic theories circulating as to the historical authenticity of the final books of *Sigurd's Lament*. Some have even gone so far as to say that my father falsified these last three books and that the recovered manuscript cut off at Book IX. This is, of course, sheer lunacy. I will not—in good conscience—even list these authors in my bibliography. I refuse to partake in academic conspiracy theories or accusations of "fake books." As everyone knows, the full and original manuscript is now on display at the Royal British Museum of History and Science. Should anyone question the document's authenticity, then I urge him or her to go and see it for him- or herself.

2. For more on the mytho-historical importance of Sigurd's name, see Byock, *Saga of the Volsungs*; Hatto, *Nibelungenlied*; Tolkien, *Legend of Sigurd and Gudrún*.

2   they are constructed
from experience's cloth,
neither factual nor real—
never fully known.
We make, we create,
and we codify.
From this, life and choice
feebly precipitate.[3]

3   High on the hill
hovering o'er the battle,
Eustace, ever vigilant,
ever Egil's scout,
stands shoulder-to-shoulder
with sturdy captain—
Magnus the bold,
but maimed warrior.[4]

4   "'Tis terrible to watch,"

3. The poet suggests that reality is a construction created from experience that can never fully be known. It was my father's contention that the poet was lamenting the mediation of language in the everyday. When I was a boy, he used to ask me: "What is a cat?" After I inevitably pointed to my family's tabby, he would ask, "Is it? Is that a cat or a *gath* or *le chat*? Who are you to say what is and is not? Words have no fixed meaning. Everything you think you know is wrong." I would, of course, sulk away like every other boy having been chastised by his father, but his point stands (he had obviously read Saussure's *Course in General Linguistics*). Language both creates and mediates reality. There is no stepping behind or through it. The poet, though saddened by this fact, also connects the way in which reality is constructed to the way in which narrative is constructed. In so doing, he enters into a long line of critical theorists (see Adams and Searle, *Critical Theory*) on the nature of poiesis. As I think of it, our fictional worlds are not so different from our empirical realities. I cannot help but wonder if they are, in fact, interchangeable. To answer that question, however, is to outpace the poet who will soon pick up that very thread with Sigurd and begin to weave a theory of both poetic and narrative construction.

4. Magnus is Egil's second in command, but apparently maimed. How? We do not know, for we cannot know. Magnus, however, means "Great" in Latin, so perhaps there is a clue after all.

he truly speaks,
"our Lord and King,
labor in combat.
Should he fall,
we should settle
on a course of action
concerned for all."[5]

5   As bright blades clash
     in battle below—
     the tug and tension
     of solitary combat—
     Magnus replies
     to his man at arms,
     with sad words
     serenely voiced:

6   "Should grim Egil
     be gutted by Alfred,
     we will work our way
     through the wood
     and return our homes
     to right order."
     Breaking his gaze
     from battle below,

7   Magnus means well,
     his moderate words:
     "We will honor the armistice
     the admirable Egil
     lawfully laid down
     with our liege lord, Alfred."[6]

5. The combat has already begun, but the poet will hide it from the reader until Book XI. For more on this poetic technique, see Walker, "Blind Reader," 11–22.

6. Magnus has chosen to honor the pact established by Alfred and Egil. Eustace, however, is Egil's spymaster and uncomfortable with Magnus' choice. For him, the pull towards freedom is too great.

Eustace, yearning for more,
yields momentarily.

8 Retiring from perch,
he roots out others,
that with whispered words
he might work his way.[7]
But Magnus, Egil's man,
implores his gods
for a miraculous miracle
manifested below.

9 He watches as warriors,
wearied Alfred and Egil,
lunge and labor
in a lurid manner.
When one is wounding,
the other is waiting,
purchasing time
with precious blood.

10 Detaining his breath
desiring divine closure,
Magnus glimpses
the finishing gore.
He fastens his eyes
'pon the flowering field
and finds fate
too fickle to follow.[8]

11 Across the pasture

---

7. My father always thought of Tolkien's Gríma Wormtongue, but that
is surely not fair to Eustace. Where Wormtongue made a career of sowing evil
and hatred, Eustace is a warrior who feels that he is doing right by his people.
He longs for freedom and neither king nor king's hand will take that from him.
Cf. Ulgik, *Of Tongues and Gods*, 123–44.

8. The *holmgang* has been decided, but the reader is, as mentioned,
blinded to the outcome.

picked for battle,
clear-headed Crispin,
Alfred's captain,
views the scene
with serene surety.[9]
Why else would Wōden
want Alfred's blade

I2 returned to Elaea,
unless to redden it
ripe and rending
with royal blood?
"Marius," he speaks,
"mayhaps today
we will spy
wondrous deeds!

I3 "What say you,
my sound lieutenant?"
"Confidence corrupts
all keen soldiers.
Today, I trust,
is for taciturn men
cautiously carrying out
their careful plans."

I4 Crispin concedes
to confidence's argument,
acknowledging wisdom
wearing knightly armor.
"Strife," he says
"in service to gods,
rarely unrolls

9. The poet leaves Egil's camp and transports us back in time to Alfred's camp, recording for us the ruminations of both Crispin and Marius. Another interesting poetic maneuver described in detail by Xanthu, "Swerve and Spin," 867–1167.

with regard to mortals."[10]

I5 "Aye and true,"
astute Marius nods.
"The gods are gracious
when gain they see,
but clearly capricious
when conflicting wants
muddle their manifested
desires 'pon mortals.[11]

I6 "Alfred, I see,
is acutely tested,
and only the future,
fickle or no,
will know the deaths
that unknot today."
Crispin, clear headed,
casts his gaze 'pon the king,

I7 "Should the splendid one
be sundered today
(though harsh words
I hesitate to speak),
what course of conduct
canst thou see?"
"The brokered bargain
between the kings

I8 "states that 'pon our sovereign
being sternly slaughtered,

---

10. Crispin believes that by fighting Umbria, Elaea is fulfilling a kind of religious service. He laments, however, that the gods rarely do as they are told. Cf. The Bible; Kaeuper, *Chivalry and Violence* and *Holy Warriors*; Hedges, *War Is a Force*; and Kay, *Lions of Al-Rassan*.

11. We are but divinity's plaything. Or perhaps the universe is nothing more than an infinite bubble in an infinity of bubbles? Cf. Greene, *Elegant Universe*; *Fabric of the Cosmos*; and *Hidden Reality*.

Umbria will from bonds release
and be boldly free
to pursue their own path,
pardoned from tribute.
Our coffers will clang
cleared of weight,

19 "but better that
than wholesale battle."
"Nay!" Crispin cried.
"Could death be so cruel
to rob us of riches
and royalty alike?"[12]
"Death cares nothing
of desires mortal.

20 "But come what may,
clear-headed Crispin,
virtue is verily
life's virginal calling.
Though second I be,
my suggestion I'll share:
honor Alfred's arrangement
and allow for pardon."[13]

21 Across the pasture
picked for battle,
as two monarchs
terribly clash,
Eustace, the Umbrian scout,
utilizes his guile
to turn fate
towards his chosen end.

12. The lamentations of empire.

13. In the line of Plato, Aristotle, and Cicero (to mention a few), Marius
lives up to his Hugoian namesake. Virtue is that to which humanity is called.
Cf. Plato, *Complete Works*; Cicero, *On Duties*; and Aristotle, *Complete Works*.

22   "Ride," he whispers
in readymade ears.
"Find Egil's son,
the successor, Sigurd,
whom remained by hearth
happily at home.
Tell him these words
though terrible to utter:

23   'Make haste through Mirkwood
with men thou trusts,
for time and destiny
unravel to-day.'
Speak sternly to Sigurd,
that stripling untested,
and send him swiftly
to survey the battle."

24   With that sly Eustace
slinks back to Magnus
to salute his lord
and sovereign chief.
"'Tis finished,"
fair-minded Magnus,
heir of Umbria,
honestly speaks.

25   "'Tis true," says Eustace,
"tidings too terrible.
For even the meanest men
find misery in defeat."
Magnus turns
too late to see
the bright blade of betrayal
bite his throat.[14]

---

14. Eustace executes Magnus in a mad gamble to defeat the Elaeans. Does
this make Eustace the Judas figure that Ernst K. Renie has made him out to

26 "To arms, to arms!"
     Eustace announces,
     'fore friends of the faithful
     can find Magnus fallen.
     And in the scurrying of time
     doth sad history
     obtain its end
     arbitrary and absolute.[15]

27 Crispin catching sight
     of the calculating Umbrians,
     shouts to Marius,
     his shrewd second:
     "Deeds shall be dutiful
     but done with regret.
     The actions of Umbria
     will be answered with war."

28 "Aye," says Marius,
     "mourn we will later.
     For now let us fight
     for fickle Jüt."[16]
     Kicking his charger,
     Marius cries:
     "To arms, to arms!
     Triumph today!"

be? Hardly! We must remember that, though despicable, Eustace's murder of Magnus is for the greater good—the end of oppression and injustice as it has been carried out by the crushing systems of Elaea. Yes, yes, this is against all of our modern sensibilities. We despise killing in the name of justice. But, perhaps, here it was necessary. Who can say? For one side of the argument, see B. J. Peters, *Through All the Plain*, and Renie, *Eustace the Traitor*, 12–19. For the other side of the argument, see Aimless, *Letter to a Drunk Scott*, and Vandergaarde, *Killing in the Name Of*, 54–68.

15. History, for the poet, is an arbitrary affair effectuated absolutely by a linear conception of time. For more, see Foucault, *Archaeology of Knowledge*.

16. Marius has been proven right. The gods are fickle, but what recourse do mortals have? Thinking thusly, he rides to battle.

29   Rushing and writhing,
      like a roiling torrent,
      the armies clash
      on that spring-crisp field.
      Where crocuses bloomed,
      now battle tramps—
      men lost to lust
      forgetting their lords.[17]

30   Woe is woven
      and to war inherent,
      as warriors wrathfully
      wound each other.
      Brother 'gainst brother—
      for bound by birth
      is not man and man
      from many wombs one?[18]

31   Some would say
      with sweet-dripped words
      that man and man
      are many and distinct.
      But who can claim,
      curt and uncaring,
      that the other is other—
      a thrashing foreigner?[19]

32   All blood is red
      and bursts when broken;
      all joy is jovial

17. Spring's expectations are ground to nothing. As my father wrote in his *Notes and Letters*: "What little hope there was in the stark, Elaean world is nothing more than an eschatological simulacra," 365.

18. The poet calls on the commonality of humankind to end its warring.

19. He rejects the notion that humankind is so different that warfare is an insignificant reality. For the poet, those who claim that foreigners are different or other are wielding nothing but "sweet-dripped words."

and rejoices at birth;
all life is loping
and lingering towards death—
So why then do we
differentiate 'tween men?[20]

33 Wōden is muffled
and Freja is mute.
Flora though fair
is fettered to fate.[21]
Little help do mortals
in their limited lives receive
when warring and lusting
and world-ordering

34 are proudly imposed
on our porous reality,[22]
we may find that we fail
for frail may we be,
but damn the gods
for damning us so.
For who are they
to throw their stones?[23]

20. To kill another, we must dehumanize, but to dehumanize is to reject the poet's truth that "all blood is red[,] all joy is jovial," and in death we are all the same. Cf. Mandela, *Long Walk to Freedom*, and Gandhi, *Autobiography*.

21. The gods are banished from the narrative.

22. Book X ends as it begins: "Both tales and truth / have this in common: / they are constructed / from experience's cloth" and "Little help do mortals / in their limited lives receive / when warring and lusting / and world-ordering / are proudly imposed / on our porous reality." In other words, from the poet's perspective there is no *a priori*.

23. Cf. John 8:7. It would be a disservice to the poet to say anything more.

Book XI

Alfred and Egil battle to death as Sigurd, gently tucked in Fjonvar, hears of war and rides to his doom.

1   Caught in the cacophony
of cruel history,
awe-inspiring Alfred,
always vigilant,
and grim-hearted Egil,
e'er genuine,
wake with the wind
that wends the sun.

2   Propelled forward
by privileged time,
arise now with aurora
radiantly ablaze!
O wondrous suns
serene to spy,
yet bringers of woe
in bright ignorance.[1]

3   Riding to reconcile
fate with remorse,
our doomed warriors

---

1. Nature is ignorant of humankind's plight.

dismount and prepare.
Unsheathing swords
and affixing shields,
two boys become tools
wielded by bureaucracy.[2]

4 Then before time
can thoroughly arrest,
the clashing and clanging
of cold steel rings forth.[3]
Bold and bloodied
do both battle:
Alfred e'er aware
of Egil's advantage,

5 Egil e'er aware
of Alfred's edge.
Gears turn for good and evil,
and though great combatants,
little either can enact
to end fate's wheel
as, bumbling through labyrinths,
the battle ends.[4]

---

2. The poet writes of kings becoming "boys." It is an interesting metamor-
phoses that here takes place, stripping the kings of their agency. They now
have no choice but to continue down the maddening tracks of war, even if they
would personally choose to exit history's train. For more on metamorphoses,
see Ovid, *Metamorphoses*.

3. Time, from our perspective, passes so quickly. Though we try and slow
it down or at times stop it completely, we are its slaves and it our master. Sci-
ence tells us differently, of course, that both time and space are manipulated
by gravity, but who among us can perceive this? What Alfred and Egil are un-
escapably wrapped in is science's indifference to humanity's perception, or is
it that science itself is a lens of perception? In what other field is the contrast
so stark as to be nearly unbelievable—what is and what is *perceived*? And yet,
in this way, theoretical science is strikingly similar to theology. Cf. Greene,
Elegant Universe; *Fabric of the Cosmos*; *Hidden Reality*; Brown, *Big History*;
Spier, *Big History*; and Christian et al., *Big History*.

4. As the battle comes to an end, the poet questions: Are we all controlled
by fate or does humanity have the free agency to act outside of its destiny?

6 Egil's edge finds Alfred
while Alfred's advantage
undoes Egil.[5]
Dropping to ground
both warriors find
their bodies expiring.
Through the sweat and ichor
found in such thronging labor,

7 Alfred speaks amused:
"Where is awareness
of such deeds undone?
Cannot I return
and call off history?"
Egil, grim to behold,
gets on his elbow
and gathers his speech:

8 "That which is done
cannot undone be.
We have doomed our nations
to despair and death,
You and I. For when—"
forgetting his words
Egil halts and heeds
his head's alarm.

9 Lying back he sees
the sea of sky
casting Elaea
in crimson hues.

While we, in our day and age, might find this ageless question tiring, the reader must remember that for the poet in his time the question of free will was all encompassing. Fate here is not some weak *deus ex machina*, but rather that which the poet feels he must both explore and wrestle with in order to make meaning from his very real, very human experience. Cf. Lots of people.

5. Killed by the other's weakness. See Howe, "Weakness as Death," 341–67.

For when kings die,
creation too laments.[6]
"Does thou see?"
he dolefully asks.

10 "Does thou see
the red-steeped heavens?"[7]
Hearing no reply,
he turns his head
and finds Alfred
finally dead.
"Hark, mine enemy,
hewn in two.

11 "I weep not for splendor
but the mortal beneath."
So saying these words
Egil slides 'cross the field
and lays his head
on his late king's breast.
Expiring thusly,
poor Egil is found

12 paying homage to potentate
he promised to kill.
Ruin is then sown
as sly Eustice upends
all that was done
by dutiful sovereigns.
Charging and clashing,
chance's armies meet

13 'pon the bed of those bound.
to battle to death.[8]

---

6. This has much in common with Luke 23:44–45, Mark 15:33, and Matt 27:51–54.

7. Who, I ask, who can read this without weeping?

8. The narrative catches up with itself as we are thrown back into Eustace's

Long was that day
of bloody labor
that resulted in rewriting
the rules of Elaea.
But before that telling,
be brought to Umbria.

14 There the first frosts
are fitfully falling
in Fjonvar's fair country
far to the north.[9]
There a fire is burning
in a fine mead hall,
Frosthelm so called
by those fierce men.[10]

15 One by the flames
now boldly sits
learning his runes
to read and write.
"Stories," he says,
"comprise my soul's work,
though with sword and shield
I am no sad slouch."[11]

16 Holding his codex
by the hearth's light,
Sigurd begins to read

perspective. The kings have slain one another and their respective armies are now clashing on the field of battle.

9. Once again, snow. See Petitt, "Snows of Sigurd."

10. Where Elaea is typified by Arthur's Camelot, Umbria can be likened to the Iceland of the Vikings, the very same one from which Egil's namesake hails. Cf. Thorsson, *Sagas of the Icelanders*, and Magnusson, *Jüt and His Country*, 47–92.

11. A world away, we find Sigurd to be more scholastic than warrior. He enjoys, we might now say, a good book and a spot of tea. He is not, in other words, your typical Viking. What transpires, however, is a very quick transformation from insulated boy to harsh, if reticent, emperor.

from that serene hall:
His bede greyhound and his brand
and no berne else
and bounes over a brode mede
with brethe at his herte.

17 *Forth he stalkes a sty*
by tho still eves,
stotays at a high street,
studyand him one.
At the sours of the sun
he sees there comand,
raikand to Rome-ward
the rediest wayes,

18 *a renk in a round clok*
with right rowme clothes[12]
both pike and palm,
als pilgrim him sholde;
the gome graithly him grette
and bade good morwen;
the king, lordly himself,
of langage of Rome,

20 *of Latin corrumped all,*
full lovely him menes:
"Wheder wilnes thou, wye,

12. Lines 3471–74 are missing. Cf. Armitage, *Death of King Arthur*, 238–41: "Then with hound and sword and no other at his side / he went fast across the fields with fury in his heart, / followed a footpath by the fringe of the forest, / then alone, by a thoroughfare, stood lost in thought. / And as the sun rose in the sky, he saw approaching, / heading toward Rome by the rapidest road, / a fellow in full cloak and flowing clothes . . . / and his staff and his palm, he appeared to be a pilgrim. / The man's greeting was a grand, 'Good morning,' / and our Sovereign responded in rough Roman speech, / gave a lordly reply in the language of Latin. / 'Wayfarer, why are you wandering here alone / with the whole world at war? Be warned, there is danger." The omitted lines read: "and a hat, and high and handsome boots. / Flattened farthings were affixed to him all over; / his hems were hung with tassels and trimmings, / and with his purse and skirted mantle, and scallop shells by the score."

walkand thine one?
Whiles this world is o war,
a wathe I it hold—[13]
Sigurd is silenced
as Frosthelm's door slams

2 1 and in walks a warrior
weary and cold.
"Hark," the herald says,
humble and kneeling,
"a time has transpired
to trash thy books
and pick up proudly
thy princely mantle.[14]

2 2 "Gather thy gear
and get thee gone
to fields below the mirk
where men now battle.
Make haste! Make haste!
For men on thee rely,
our proud prince no longer,
now our principle crown."

---

13. Sigurd is here reading from Benson's, *King Arthur's Death*. This, of course, places *Sigurd's Lament* both in its historical and literary context. It is as if the poet is here paying deference to his betters, though he might have added Tolkien's *Lay of the Children of Húrin* to his list. Cf. Tolkien, *Lays of Beleriand*, 1–125, "In fear woke Túrin, / and a form he guessed / o'er his body bending / with blade naked / His death or torment / he deemed was come, / . . . Lo! the bonds were burst / that had bound his hands / . . . he flung him fiercely / on the foe he dreamed, / and Beleg falling / breathless earthward / was crushed beneath him / . . . by the help of doom; / at the throat he thrust; / through he pierced it, / that the blood was buried / in the blood-wet mould; / . . . 'A! madness damned! / with friends thou fightest!'. . . stone-faced he stood / staring frozen / on that dreadful death, / and his deed knowing / wildeyed he gazed / with waking horror, / as in endless anguish / an image carven."

14. We do not know who this messenger is, but a king, he claims, does not read. A king wars. Compare with Alfred's guide throughout Avalonia in Book II or his relationship to Flora in Books III–V.

23 "What are these words
that thou recklessly speaks?
I am no sure sovereign
but the son of king living."[15]
"Would that were true
and wondrous miracles prevailed,
but mine lord is dead,
long live my lord."

24 "How?" Sigurd asks,
with surging anger.
"'Twas Alfred that truant
who awoke in time
and challenged thy king
to solitary combat."
"My father died fighting
that foreign crown?"[16]

25 "Aye," barks the herald,
"but it's time to be gone.
Eustace the true
has taken charge,
but battle is capricious
and can boldly adapt.
Warriors need their king
and a king needs his warriors."

26 "Might I a moment
to mourn my father?
He was good and gracious,
and gained my respect."
"Nay, young monarch,
now's not the moment.

15. Sigurd, until the end, is reluctant to take on his new role. That is, of course, his internal struggle. Will he become that which he despises? Cf. Bombadil, "Sigurd's Choice," 56–90.

16. Much has been written on Sigurd's response to the death of his father. See Hurtlock, *Encyclopedia of Psychoanalysis and the Sigurd Complex.*

Time 'tis fast
and faster yet.

27 "History forces choice
that few find consoling,
but men of action
must move with speed."[17]
So saying, the herald stood
to survey the lodge.
"Away good lord, away,
for our answer must
            with vengeance come."

28 Swiftly through mirkwood
does the sovereign travel,
questioning his companions
on his current quest.
Arriving at truth
as it is accounted to him,
he holds Elaea responsible
for his author's repose.

29 A savage spite
suddenly surges,
for loss and lament
would the Elaeans pay.
But in the liminal,
that linking wood,
where thin is the space
separating god and mortal,[18]

---

17. In life, the messenger claims, we are given choices, and the bold must make them without regret.

18. For this one, brief moment does Sigurd have access to the divine. Upon Alfred's return to Elaea, you may recall, interaction with the gods was cut off. Here, however, we see Flora (presumably) return to dissuade Sigurd from his present course. Interestingly, where the gods could move freely throughout Elaea in the first part of the book, here they require a liminal space in order to make their whispers known. Cf. van Gennep, *Rites of Passage.*

30 Sigurd hears whispers
and supernal sighs:
"The urge to bleed
for Umbrians is hard,
but to master desires
is the master task.[19]
Does thou thrive
'pon thirsty blades

31 or sheathing swords
for ending strife?
The choice is thine
but choose thee well,
for the grinding stones
of sorrowful history
once set in motion
cannot unset be."[20]

32 The voice finishes
as fair Sigurd crosses
from thin to thick,
from serene to thunderous.[21]
Taking in the battle,
his boyhood sings
overcome with confidence
calling his blood.[22]

33 He raises an arm,
reaching to heaven,
and screams with spittle

19. It would appear that Flora—or whoever the divine whisperer might be—is a Stoic. For the best in Stoic thought, see Aurelius, *Meditations*, 1.

20. And so it appears that history lays at the feet of a boy king. It is his choice that will decide the fate of Elaea. Will he go to war or will he stop the madness? Will call for peace or revolution? Will he serve or end his kingdom's servitude?

21. He has left the liminal, and the voice of the god is once more silent.

22. And what should decide for him, but his adolescence!

escaping his jaw:
"How dare the gods
deem me weak
and ask me to stay
my surfeited wrath.

34 "Below me my birth-lord
lingers in Hel
and I to his honor
will hew limb from limb."
So saying and cursing,
Sigurd rides to his doom,
slaying mortals whose sin
was but to serve their lord.[23]

23. Here we see the arbitrariness of war. Sigurd is overcome with both the lure of war and desire of avenging his father. He is doing nothing more than falling under the sway of his culture's mythologies. But, the poet points out, those whom he kills are not his enemies, but rather those that are only guilty of following their liege-lord into battle. And is not that the way of it? Our kings and presidents stay warmly at home while the young and poor bleed in our wars, killing and dying for ideologies and myths.

Book XII

The final book in which the fate of Elaea is laid bare by the blade of Sigurd.

I The dawn brings hope and despair alike
when after weary battle the wet field is combed.[1]
But that is for scavengers and slaves to sate
and not young Sigurd, our monarch of Gotland,
who now freshly settled sits in intricate silence
listening to loons in a nearby lake.
The haunting calls hang in the air
and pierces deep the potentate's pneuma.[2]
      Nature
    is never neutral
    but verily violent,
    and though it be brutal
    it is serene in silence.

---

1. Books that should be read, but in no particular order: Bulgakov, *Master and Margarita*; Meloy, *Wildwood*; Robinson, *Gilead*; Russell, *The Sparrow*; Vaughan, *Saga*, vol. 1; Eco and Martini, *Belief or Nonbelief?*; Edmundson, *Why Read?*; Stewart, *Crystal Cave*; Mulisch, *Discovery of Heaven*; Borg and Wright, *Meaning of Jesus*; Yorke, *Into the Woods*; Jewett, *Romans*; Rothfuss, *Name of the Wind*; Aslan, *Zealot*; Kazantzakis, *Last Temptation of Christ*; Dostoevsky, *Brothers Karamazov*; Geertz, *Interpretation of Cultures*; Hoopes, *Peirce on Signs*.

2. The battle is over.

2   "My soul quakes," young Sigurd speaks,[3]
    "when I went to war I rode in anger.
    I bumbled through battle as a bringer of death.
    I hacked and hewed and Hel I wrought,
    but now I find my father buried
    and in his place I will be placed.
    Such sickness is sought in the slicing melee,
    a wrath revealed in the wonderment of
         cosmos.
      Philosophers play
      at unknotting knowledge,
      but by that betray
      our constructed collage.[4]

3   "For this is truth, terrible and yawning:
    all we mold and pretend to master
    is the present matter, a primordial motion
    crashing and clanging and canceling progress.
    We pretend and profess that history is pointed,
    but victory is random and rarely righteous
    and to rule is to descend into deeper deceit.
    But who am I to reject with ambivalence
         the honor
      brightly bestowed
      by great Gotland
      and that freely flowed
      from honest hands?[5]

4   "I am no king, yet crowned I am.
    I am no leader, yet learned I am.
    I am no tactician, yet told I am
    that my bold blueprint bore the day.

3. The lament begins.

4. For Sigurd, all we know or can know is comprised of human experience. There is nothing outside that allows for a greater narrative. He asks, lamenting, why this is so and if he has the freedom to write his own story?

5. History is arbitrary, but tradition is not. Sigurd cannot reject the lore of generations in favor of his youthful whims.

So with these words I readily wield
I must worry my way towards true awareness.
Youth my young guide you'll no longer serve
as mine cool companion careening towards duty.
>   Be gone!
>   Find another fool
>   'pon which to prey
>   for a relinquished rule
>   is insolent to stay."[6]

5   So saying he stands to seize his crown
when a wind rushes up and whips his tent.
The flaps fly open as furtive Eustice,
now the king's captain, coasts into view.
"Hail," he speaks surly and sly,
"a storm is surfacing, streaming from the north.
So the king's coronation must soon commence,
so that our siege of that Elaean city
>   might
>   continue apace."[7]
>   Finished and formal,
>   he bows his bold face,
>   e'er ready and resourceful.[8]

6. Shucking off youth and grabbing hold of his future, Sigurd's lament comes to an end. Much has been written on these three stanzas and why the name of the poem should point us here for its meaning. For more, see Lanthny, *How Deserted Lies the City*, 78–321.

7. The Umbrians have been victorious in battle and the city's defenses are no doubt in want. Eustace here calls Sigurd to finish what his father had started and strike a grievous blow to Elaea once and for all. In order for this to mean anything, however, Sigurd must first be consecrated to the Umbrian's gods or God (some believe that it is the Elaeans that are pagan and the Umbrians that are Christian). See H. B. Peters, *Religion*, 237.

8. I fought off that . . . beast. "The guardian," it called itself. Well, it's gone now. I am alone and prying up the floorboard marked "4–5–s." I'm peering into the darkness. I see . . . no . . . wait . . . I see . . . a bottle . . . yes . . . and . . . a note. I pull it up. There . . . in the bottle. X–x–8. All of the clues: Abe45sxx8. Ha! That old bastard. It's here. Yes. *Here.* And a note. "I'm sorry," it says. "I'm sorry."

6 Stepping outside to his stern soldiers,
   Sigurd, as all sure kings are certain to do,
   knelt 'fore his priest now prepared for pageantry.
   "Gods," the cleric calls, "are cruel in their ways,
   but true to northmen who nurture their rites.
   Abstain not from ablutions divine
   and ne'er forego the defense of faith.
   The south might be rich in e'er sweet bounty,
        but a sovereign's
     terrible task
     is to royally refrain
     from sin's sleek mask
     while the philistines slaying."[9]

7 "Are thou able to acknowledge these laws?"
   "Aye," sighs Sigurd, stacked with burden.
   "Then arise anew as Avalonia's sovereign
   and lead us to slaughter lowly men now abed."[10]
   Eustace then claps his king on the shoulder,
   "Now is the time to triumph o'er this city.
   For too long has 'laea lingered in comfort,
   pushing and pedaling its painted philosophy.[11]
        Slaves
     no longer, but lords we are.
     Warriors of renown
     and sophisticated saviors
     soon to clutch Elaea's crown."[12]

---

9. The religious call here is to recall virtue and then kill without losing that virtue. Paradoxical indeed. See H. B. Peters, *Religion*, and B. J. Peters, *Through All the Plain*.

10. Violence is here motivated by religion, yes, but also politics and economics. Perhaps our categories are unfair? Cf. Asad, *Formations of the Secular* and *Genealogies of Religion*; Armstrong, *Fields of Blood*; and Said, *Orientalism*.

11. "Painted" should be taken to mean "surface," "shallow," or "materialistic."

12. How we love to fool ourselves!

8 "Form the men," feeble Sigurd says,[13]
"and prepare the assault on that once prime city.
In the vanguard I'll valiantly ride
for little to fear do the fated have."
Soon hosts are mounted surrounding the walls,
and pawing the soil prepared for the charge.
Sigurd sits serenely surveying the field,
a newly crowned king called to battle.

> Ripping
> from sheath his saber
> he launches the labor
> that hard history
> will memorize as misery.

9 Then open the skies 'pon pitiful Elaea,
shackling spring to secure winter's hold.
Bursting and blowing, bitter snow careens
towards hurtling warriors terrible to behold.[14]
Wet and weary, the watch observes
mad men of the north marauding and murderous.
Blowing the horn, the bright note of alarm,
the gate is closing with a great scurry.

> Too late
> was the plan performed
> as covert and cunning
> Sigurd's spies swiftly storm
> and execute their cutting.[15]

10 The watch now dead, the way lies open
for angry men to sow angry deeds.
Long is that lay of 'lea's sacking
and elsewhere sung with sophistication and style.
That poet of poets propelled by passion

---

13. Why the epithet "feeble?" See Boron, *Sigurd's Madness*, 34.

14. Snow!

15. Led by Eustace, no doubt.

chose that topic for her truest creation.[16]
Who am I, an anonymous teller,
to bring profit where profits already been won?
>No,
>>I'll not trod that trail
>>so elegantly effectuated,
>>for the tale I'd tell
>>would acutely attenuate.[17]

I I Rather I'll sing of Sigurd's last song,
the culmination of choices so crucially made.
The city was won, if reduced to rubble,
but there stands Sigurd 'fore the sturdy throne.
Filling with doubt at so dreadful a claim,
the boy-king muses beyond his years:[18]
"What is a chair to champion such fear?
Do I not deserve it for my dreadful deeds?
>Aye!
>>is the apt answer
>>so generously given,
>>but to command is a cancer
>>in a realm so riven.[19]

I 2 "And the vaunted ceilings viewed from below
are ready-made reminders of royalty's insignificance.[20]

---

16. Mysterious indeed, the poet claims that the sack of Elaea has been recorded elsewhere by a female poet that he refers to as "the poet of poets." We can only guess at who this poet is or what her poem included, but sadly both are lost to time.

17. Why mess with what has already been done and by a better mind no less?

18. And here is Sigurd's third reflection on who he is and why he should not be king.

19. How will he ever repair the damage done to Elaea? How will he ever forge one kingdom from two?

20. Architecture is often said to pull our minds towards greater things—hopeful things. Sigurd, however, sees it as a constant reminder that below the gods we must all look as ants, kings and plebeians alike. Cf. Foucault, *Discipline and Punish*, 195–230.

Humanity, to be sure, when heaped together
is able to accomplish the awe-inspiring,
but one alone always will fail
and find that fate is fickle indeed.
Mine enemies surround and know my weakness.
How then can I sit as a sure sovereign
       Upon
    that gilded grace
    when I made war
    with murderous pace
    'pon the domain I once deplored?

I3   "And yet priests proudly proclaim my right
given by the gods to govern Elaea.
But who are gods to grant such privilege?
With mere mortals do they mean to speak?
Nay! Nothing but silence and naught but sorrow
do they condescendingly cultivate 'pon earth.[21]
They do not deign to declare themselves to me!
So why should I surrender to the celestial?
      Reason
    is my sharp sword
    stropped by stories,
    a refined reward
    but constant quarry.[22]

I4   "There it is, that throne thick and heavy,
good and golden, great to behold.
Yet pearled with peril and with oppression forged.
It is singly a sign signifying power.
And what is a sign? A sure thing that lies?
Or something else by something else?
'Tis a simulacra situated in the mind,
a meaningless thing made for power
        and control,

21. Such a different experience than Alfred's.

22. Why listen to or seek out the gods? Sigurd has both his reasons and narratives. Such suffices, yes?

with which I'll work
the right and true
knitting kingdoms
to make matter anew.[23]

I 5 "Time draws swiftly," Sigurd whispers.
"I must assume the mantle, master of all.
No more elusion elicited by hope,
for cares will conclude with the chronicles of history.
May what's written recall the virtue
and by scribes and scholars be sound and just."[24]
So saying does Sigurd stride to the throne
and sit 'pon that surety sealing his fate.
      Hark!
    All rise for royalty,
    the emperor of Elaea.
    The king is dead,
    long live the king.

I 6 Sung, O Bard, thou sat and told,[25]
of that benevolent hero who bid his life.[26]
Who ascended to Avalonia and arose in grief
while despairing the death of his dear kindred.

23. On signs and their ability to lie, see Eco, *Theory of Semiotics*; *Semiotics and the Philosophy of Language*; *Baudolino*; Hoopes, *Peirce On Signs*; and Moore, *Charles S. Peirce*.

24. He has made his choice. May the historians be kind.

25. And so the poem begins as it ends: "Sing, O Bard, / sit and tell, / of benevolent hero / bidding life."

26. Yes, I came back. Despite the alcoholism, the abuse, and the way in which he treated my mother. I came back and, alongside him, worked on his translation of *Sigurd's Lament*. He died a year later, of course, but we were able to finish the translation and make good headway into his academic apparatus. That which he could not or did not want to finish, I have taken it upon myself to complete. But why? Why? I had left. I had said my goodbyes. So why did I return? Why did I move my family and children back to London? It was what he had said to me on the phone. We had not communicated in years, of course, and so it came out of nowhere when I received an email from my mother saying: "He's calling. Pick up." So I did. And he said . . . he said.

Sad 'twas sung and sorrowfully waxed
of Edward's cloak crimson stained
by Gotlander's grim offspring who Gramarye's truce broke
and reaped a doom reversed by none.
    In lament
    thou sung so well
    of divine deity,
    heroism in Hel,
    and the unseen seen.

17 Sung, O Bard, thou sat and told,
of Sigurd's actions, afterwards wrought:
of marching on Caerpel, of marauders besetting,
of loved ones low-brought, and of lurid transgressions.
Scribe thou did score, thou did set in runes,
that song once sung—Sigurd's Lament.
Now call on thy muse and compel us towards virtue
for a song once sung 'tis sung forever:[27]
    May you,
    mine hearts and hearers
    who bear history's burdens,
    triumph o'er tyrannical error
    and evil ever determined.[28]

27. "Manuscripts don't burn." Cf. Bulgakov, *Master and Margarita*.

28. The poet shifts from invoking the "bard" to the "muse," though whom either are is a mystery. He ends the poem with a benediction calling his readers to triumph over history, yes, but also those forces and powers that manipulate history towards their evil ends. This can only be read as a veiled condemnation of the political, economic, and religious leaders of his age, those who would endlessly choose ideology over humanity. Cf. Pope Francis, *Evangelii Gaudium*, and Crantzi, *In the Arms of Tyranny We Rise*, 78–89.

Appendix A

Wallace Walker Peters' Unpublished Paper on Distention

DISTENDED RECEPTION: MEANING CONSTRUCTION WITHIN HERMENEUTICAL CLUSTERS

Introduction

The reader is always tainted by first encounters, which bothers me more than it should. Why? Because I read fiction, a lot of fiction, and try as I might to compartmentalize, I recently realized that I do academia in concert with fiction—that I filter the academic through the fictional. For me, this has led to an ambiguity of interpretation and a realization that I always read and interpret according to my own literary history. It is this ambiguity that I seek to understand by introducing three separate but entangled concepts: distended reception (the act of stretching out into both the past and future), injected narratives (the initial point of ritual theory), and hermeneutical clusters (a kind of cultural encyclopedia similar to that of Umberto Eco's). The blending of fiction and academia, of forcing a literary history into a chronological history is, for me, exemplified in a statement made by Paul Ricoeur. There is an incongruous confrontation, Ricoeur argues, between Aristotle and Augustine, concordance and discordance, time and narrative. A confrontation that is "all the more incongruous in that it goes from Augustine to Aristotle, contrary to the chronological order."[1] If I am interested in anything, then it is that—all of that—which is contrary to the chronological order.

To briefly summarize and spoil the end: If distended reception is the process of any text blooming throughout literary history into the past and future, then the first step of limiting this proliferation is the notion or concept of the injected narrative. The second step is interpreting any injected narrative through the hermeneutical cluster. It is this dynamic event—the interaction and exchange between the injected narrative and hermeneutical cluster—that allows us to say something meaningful concerning the texts about which we so deeply care.[2]

Distended Reception

> Time is nothing other than a stretching out, but of what I don't know; it would be surprising if it were not a stretching out of my own mind.[3]

We are caught in the inescapable present. What is future slips by into that which is now past. As we reach for or grasp after fixed points, we find ourselves stretched thin, trying to remember. But the present consciousness is pulled in two directions—future and past—stymieing us at every turn. When our attention is on the present "the future is transferred to become the past."[4] Imagine a person singing a hymn. The hymnal lies open before her. The music plays. She begins. Earnestly doing her best, she focuses on what is to come but only within the context of holding in her mind what has past. In this way, the present flows without her ever having grabbed ahold of it. As Augustine described this sensation: "A person singing or listening to a song [s]he knows well suffers a distension or stretching in feeling and in sense perception from

1. Ricoeur, *Time and Narrative*, 1:3.
2. Gadamer, *Truth and Method*, 479.
3. Nightingale, *Once Out of Nature*, 79.
4. Augustine, *Confessions*, 243.

the expectation of future sounds and the memory of past sound."[5] But suppose this is not only true for singing? "It is also valid," Augustine continues, "of the entire life of an individual person, where all actions are parts of a whole, and of the total history of 'the sons of men' where all human lives are but parts."[6]

The difficulty with distension is that it makes us extremely uncomfortable. We want to believe that we are the master of time and place, that we have set boundaries that allow us to know things and engage reality. But perhaps we are slaves to our conceptions of time and distension and all that we know—all of our knowledge constructions and disciplines—are heuristics for a grasping humanity. Distension is interesting then because it allows for the engagement of texts in new, fresh ways, ways that instigate the processes of interpretation and understanding. But what is an Augustinian distension when applied to literature?

Simply put, distended reception is the study of first isolating a text and then examining how it stretches in two directions—the past and the future. To take the *Aeneid* as a representative example: we know its genre as epic poetry. We know that it came after the *Iliad* and *Odyssey*, but before *The Divine Comedy*. We like to believe that there is a nice and tidy chain of receptive influences running through time from one to the other. But if we were to look at the *Aeneid* alone, then we quickly see that it not only shapes *our* reading of Dante, but also *our* reading of Homer, if not Homer himself.[7] The process of distension then is the examination of a particular text's stretching into the past and the future, it is exploring both its before-texts and its after-texts, and the way in which the past (Homer), present (Virgil), and future (Dante) are all in mutual relationship with one another.

By way of contrast, reception theory studies the way in which a text has been received throughout its life or the way a text has moved down the corridors of chronological history. We are more than comfortable with this approach. "The literature of the past,"

5. Ibid., 245.
6. Ibid., 243, and Ps 30:20.
7. Cf. Graf, "Myth in Ovid," 110.

Ernst Robert Curtius posits, "can always be active in that of the present."[8] But what if a text distends? What if it moves out into both the past and the future, rearranging our understanding of the text or texts? "As much as the present is directed by the past," T. S. Eliot argues, "the past should be altered by the present."[9] This idea of distended reception then, reminds us that while texts have historical locations, they are not only historically located. They move out in two ways, engaging the past and the future, their before-texts and after-texts, which "involves a unique co-existence of past and present" and future.[10] In this way, texts are always in the process of being consulted, engaged, and redrawn in a process of distended reception. My reading of Virgil shapes my reading of Dante shapes my reading of Homer shapes my reading of Virgil.

"Any text," Julia Kristeva writes, "is constructed as a mosaic of quotations; any text is the absorption and transformation of another."[11] At first glance, while distended reception is focused on the text and its distention (much like Kristeva's intertextuality), distended reception is better viewed as seeking to understand how the role a reader, her interpretive community, and the infinite web of textual interconnections are entangled in the life of any text. The focus of distended reception then is on both the interplay of intertextuality and the reader or reading community that employs her or their own collection of quotations.

Helpful here in carving out distention's unique space is Pierre Bayard's notion of literary history. Bayard suggests that literary history and chronological history are not the same, and that writers and artists partake of a dual chronology. In this new domain of literary history, the *after* may be situated *before* the before.[12] As an example, I read Dante before Virgil and, though contrary to the chronological order, my literary history is vastly different from that of the chronological. I cannot help but read Virgil through

8. Curtius, *European Literature and the Latin Middle Ages.*

9. Eliot, "Tradition and the Individual Talent," 39.

10. Gadamer, *Truth and Method,* 408.

11. Kristeva, *Desire in Language,* 66.

12. Bayard, "Anticipatory Plagiarism," 231–50.

Dante now. What Bayard takes for granted, however, is that dual chronology is—*de facto*—a function of literature. Whereas distended reception opens us to the wonderful process of Augustine's distention, it also shows us *how* Bayard's dual chronology functions and provides us a methodology for further research.

It is here that we must insert Umberto Eco into the conversation. Texts are signs. A sign's *content*, not its *referent*, is its meaning. These content laden signs are what Eco calls "cultural units,"[13] which exist as essential parts of any world-vision belonging to any particular culture.[14] Echian cultural units are best viewed as elements in a system of other cultural units, limiting or further defining any other cultural units' meaning.[15] Eco's cultural unit provides us with a philosophical explanation for Augustine's statement: "[Distention] is also valid for the entire life . . . where all actions are parts of a whole, and of the total history of [humanity] where all human lives are but parts."[16] Once a text exists as a cultural unit then, it enters into a cultural relationship with other cultural units. It is these content laden, cultural units that exist in Bayard's literary history, *bloom* outwards in space and time, and shape the way in which we read both the future and the past. Without Eco's cultural unit, we have little with which to work.[17]

In summary, a text, once written—or perhaps conceived?—exists as a cultural unit that enters into a complex web or encyclopedia[18] of relationality with other cultural units. In this cultural nexus, a text breaks off into literary history and can move either forwards or backwards or multidimensionally within chronological time. This movement is analogous to a bloom—a blossoming

13. Eco, *Theory of Semiotics*, 66–68, and *Semiotics and the Philosophy of Language*, 46–86. See also Desogus, "Encyclopedia in Umberto Eco's Semiotics," 506–8.

14. Eco, *Theory of Semiotics*, 79–80.

15. Ibid., 73.

16. Augustine, *Confessions*, 243.

17. Cf. Genette, *Palimpsests*, 1–5. Genette's conception of "transtextuality" is helpful in conceiving of this process, but his *hypo-* to *hyper-* is too limiting in its scope.

18. Eco, *Semiotics and the Philosophy of Language*, 46–86.

or blurring—within multidimensional space that can neither be accounted for nor controlled. Given any text then, we can arrive at any other text and "any single interpretation" cannot be "correct 'in itself.'"[19] This is Ricoeur's contrary to the chronological order, which is all the more dramatic, he claims, as it is "in the mind of one and the same reader."[20] And yet, what does this leave us with but the distasteful proliferation of meaning—vast, overwhelming, and, yes, a little depressing? Against this backdrop of a cultural web in which significance is arbitrary and fixed texts are disrupted, how can we make claims about texts in ways that matter?

Injected Narratives

> The creation of "as if" worlds is a central aspect of ritual
> action, which we see as necessary for human life.[21]

Through *borrowing* an important concept from ritual theory—the initial act—we can begin to answer the question: how can we make claims about texts in ways that matter? The initial act provides us with a structure for ordering our everyday experiences[22] that are otherwise random and uncertain. The initial act or injected narrative becomes a necessary condition around which a hermeneutical cluster can arise, which then inaugurates the rules of any particular community's interpretive and embodying game.

Please allow me a short, poetic detour: "Nature displayed a single aspect only / throughout the cosmos," Ovid writes, "Chaos was its name."[23] This chaos was neither good nor bad. It was only chaos: "disconnected elements all heaped / together in anarchic disarray."[24] Chaos is, however, incomprehensible without order,

19. Gadamer, *Truth and Method*, 415.

20. Ricoeur, *Time and Narrative*, 1:4.

21. Seligman, *Ritual and Its Consequences*, 25.

22. The move from text to "everyday experiences" will, hopefully, become clear, though hermeneutics as the science of interpretation blurs these boundaries. Cf. Schleiermacher, *Hermeneutics*, 67.

23. Ovid, *Metamorphoses*, 15.

24. Ibid.

and so a narrative was injected into perception in order to compre-
hend the otherwise pandemoniacal.[25] This narrative is nameless.
It has no meaning itself. It is and can be anything, so long as it is
injected *a priori* into human experience. "Mortal men are afraid,"
Ovid's predecessor, Lucretius claims, "as they look about them and
see / the many things that happen on earth and up in the sky, /
and they cannot tell why or how and therefore think that gods /
must bring them about by fiat."[26] Some inject their own narratives.
Some claim to have it injected for them. In some ways then, the in-
jected narrative is reminiscent of the "initial act" or "presupposed
starting point" of ritual theory that is "instituted by a superhuman
agent."[27]

     In other words, we looked out into infinity and were over-
come by the terrible expanse of the natural world.[28] It dwarfed our
expectations and diminished our hopes of being the epicenter. So
we injected an initial act into history, in order to fix a point in
time by which our experiences could be measured. As Ovid sum-
marizes it: "Who would believe this, if it were not sanctioned by
antiquity?"[29] This narrative, once injected, becomes a structure to
reality and experiences that functions to order the vast chaos of all
that was and is.

     Religion, for obvious reasons, is easy prey. Much harder is
science. "Wonderful as it is," Marcelo Gleiser, a theoretical physi-
cist at Dartmouth, writes, "science is a human construction, a nar-
rative we create to make sense of the world around us."[30] For him,
the grand injection of the theoretical scientific community is the
"Ionian Enchantment" of oneness—the search for unification as
best represented by string theorists. It is a scientific monotheism, if
you like, that provides its representatives a fixed point upon which
to hang their hat of meaning.

25. Milton, *Paradise Lost*, II:890–920.

26. Lucretius, *De Rerum Natura*, 7.

27. Lawson, "Cognition," 83.

28. Lucretius, *De Rerum Natura*, 41.

29. Graf, "Myth in Ovid," 120.

30. Gleiser, *Tear at the Edge of Creation*, 6.

But why pick on science? For two reasons: one, to show that we all inject narratives into our experience, not only the "believer." And two, because it is a thing that we so often take for granted. In our day and age, science and its constituent parts are both god and monarch, creating and ruling over our empirical and economic powers of knowledge. For us, science is *a priori*, foundational, *ex nihilo*. And yet, Hans-Georg Gadamer writes, "the truth that science states is itself relative to a particular world orientation and cannot at all claim to be the whole."[31] If science in the modern world injects a unifying narrative into our experience, then it reveals our desperate need for order and structure in a life riddled with distended reception. To put it differently,[32] the injected narrative is the first step in ordering the chaotic and arbitrary. It is inescapable. It is the drive to inject an *a priori*—a presupposed starting point—against which to measure our experiences. If distended reception reveals a proliferation of meaning and the injected narrative is the first step in limiting that proliferation, then the second step, to which we now turn, is the cluster of texts by which we interpret any injected narrative.

Hermeneutical Cluster and Meaning Creation

> Thus here it really is true to say that this event is not our action upon the thing, but the act of the thing itself.[33]

A hermeneutical cluster is the particular web of texts that any individual or community wields in order to interpret their chosen injected narrative. It is through the hermeneutical cluster, interacting with its injected narrative, that we are able to say anything meaningful about texts. It is helpful to think of a hermeneutical cluster like a bibliography or Friedrich Schleiermacher's "hermeneutic

31. Gadamer, *Truth and Method*, 465.

32. The injected narrative—no matter how fruitless—is the concerted effort to master another thinker's distention, that of Jacques Derrida's différance and deferral—those present absences, those unknown-known forces that endlessly differ meaning. Derrida, "Différance," 129–60.

33. Gadamer, *Truth and Method*, 479.

canon"[34] or Eco's encyclopedia.[35] It is the grouping of texts that you or your community employs in order to make sense of or interpret an injected narrative. The hermeneutical cluster, however, is a cluster and neither bibliography nor canon nor encyclopedia. It is a "cluster" as it implies a web of interconnected, relational, and dynamic connections, and a "text" as it implies any cultural unit that is put into relationship with any other cultural unit.

It is the hermeneutical cluster then that establishes a community's rules of interpretation or embodiment—how to both think and live in the world. It is through the hermeneutical cluster that a community arrives at orthodoxy, heterodoxy, or heresy, as well as its praxis counterparts. And it is the hermeneutical cluster that allows any community to make sense of the world, yes, but also to define, confine, and other.

The rules of interpretation and embodiment created by any hermeneutical cluster in relationship with any injected narrative are analogous to the rules of any particular game. These rules of interpretation and embodiment are established in scientific communities, in academia, in nation-states, and in religions. "We interpret and embody this way," we say, "and not that way—not like them. They've got it all wrong." Based on what? On the rules of a particular game constructed from a particular hermeneutical cluster. The rules through which any community interprets, as arbitrary as they might be, allow for the saying of something meaningful. The game can differ, of course, from community to community, but so too can the rules, given the same game. Two communities might have the same injected narrative, but as they bring different hermeneutical clusters to bear on that narrative, their interpretations and embodiments will vary.

In summary, if distended reception is the process of any text blooming throughout literary history into the past and future, then the first step of limiting that proliferation is the notion or concept of the injected narrative. The second step is interpreting any injected narrative through the hermeneutical cluster. It is this dynamic

34. Schleiermacher, *Hermeneutics*, 64.

35. Eco, *Semiotics and the Philosophy of Language*, 46–86.

event—the interaction and exchange between the injected narrative and hermeneutical cluster—that allows us to say something meaningful concerning the texts about which we so deeply care.

Conclusion

I began by saying that I do academia in concert with fiction—that I filter the academic through the fictional. For me, this has led to an ambiguity of interpretation and a realization that I always read and interpret according to my own literary history. Through presenting the ideas of distended reception, injected narratives, and hermeneutical clusters, I hope to have navigated and come to a better understanding of this ambiguity.

In the end, this paper—all of our papers—are about the authors we have read, engaged, and reread (and perhaps even those authors that we do not admit to reading). Underlying each study, project, or paper is a web of interconnected texts blooming out in a multidimensional literary history. Ricoeur, yes, but also J. R. R. Tolkien, the Bible, and Chinua Achebe shape me. My literary history knows little of hierarchies, preferences, or canons until I have injected a narrative and interpreted it through a hermeneutical cluster. All texts seem to impinge then and care little for chronology. To sort them out, to isolate them, is that which I do according to an arbitrary set of rules extracted from a hermeneutical cluster that is dynamically seeking to manipulate an injected narrative. In this way, and contrary to the chronological order, I am able to say something meaningful concerning the texts about which I so deeply care.

Appendix B

Bibliography to Wallace Walker Peters'
Unpublished Paper on Distention

Augustine. *Confessions.* Translated by Henry Chadwick. Oxford: Oxford University Press, 1991.

Bayard, Pierre. "Anticipatory Plagiarism." Translated by Jeffrey Mehlman. *New Literary History* 44 (2013) 231–50.

Curtius, E. R. *European Literature and the Latin Middle Ages.* Translated by Willard R. Trask. New York: Routledge, 1953.

Derrida, Jacques. "Differance." In *Speech and Phenomena, and Other Essays on Husserl's Theory of Signs,* 129–60. Evanston, IL: Northwestern University Press, 1973.

Desogus, Paolo. "The Encyclopedia in Umberto Eco's Semiotics." *Semiotica* 192 (2012) 501–21.

Eco, Umberto. *Semiotics and the Philosophy of Language.* Bloomington: Indiana University Press, 1986.

———. *A Theory of Semiotics.* Bloomington: Indiana University Press, 1979.

Eliot, T. S. "Tradition and the Individual Talent." In *Selected Prose of T. S. Eliot,* edited by Frank Kermode, 37–44. New York: Farrar, Straus and Giroux, 1975.

Gadamer, Hans-Georg. *Truth and Method.* Translated by Joel Weinsheimer and Donald G. Marshall. Rev. ed. London: Bloomsbury, 2013.

Genette, Gérard. *Palimpsests: Literature in the Second Degree.* Translated by Channa Newman and Claude Doubinsky. Lincoln: University of Nebraska Press, 1997.

Gleiser, Marcelo. *A Tear at the Edge of Creation: A Radical New Vision for Life in an Imperfect Universe.* New York: Free Press, 2010.

Graf, Fritz. "Myth in Ovid." In *The Cambridge Companion to Ovid,* edited by Philip Hardie, 108–21. Cambridge: Cambridge University Press, 2002.

Kristeva, Julia. *Desire in Language: A Semiotic Approach to Literature and Art.* New York: Columbia University Press, 1980.

Lawson, E. Thomas. "Cognition." In *Guide to the Study of Religion*, edited by Willi Braun and Russell T. McCutcheon. London: Cassell, 2000.

Lucretius. *De Rerum Natura (The Nature of Things)*. Translated by David R. Slavitt. Berkeley: University of California Press, 2008.

Milton, John. *Paradise Lost*. Edited by Alastair Fowler. London: Pearson Longman, 2007.

Nightingale, Andrea. *Once Out of Nature: Augustine on Time and the Body*. Chicago: University of Chicago Press, 2011.

Ovid. *Metamorphoses*. Translated by Charles Martin. New York: Norton, 2004.

Ricoeur, Paul. *Time and Narrative*. Translated by Kathleen McLaughlin and David Pellauer. Vol. 1. Chicago: University of Chicago Press, 1984.

Schleiermacher, Friedrich. *Hermeneutics and Criticism and Other Writings*. Cambridge: Cambridge University Press, 1998.

Seligman, Adam B., et al. *Ritual and Its Consequences: An Essay on the Limits of Its Sincerity*. Oxford: Oxford University Press, 2008.

Appendix C

Figure 1A: Wallace Walker Peters'
Unpublished Diagram of Distention

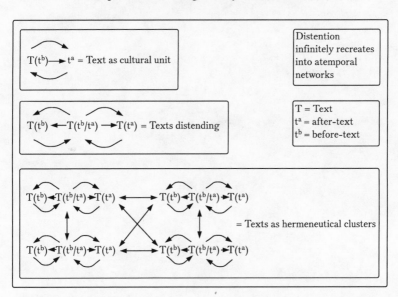

Bibliography

Adams, Hazard, and Leroy Searle. *Critical Theory since Plato*. Boston: Cengage Learning, 2004.

Aimless, Bradbury W. *Letter to a Drunk Scott: An Inkling of Hope*. Cambridge: Cambridge University Press, 2005.

Ajani, Lance F. "Warmhurst Is Wrong." *Journal for Sigurd Studies* 12 (2014) 113–56.

Aland, Barbara, et al. *The Greek New Testament*. Stuggart: Deutsche Bibelgesellschaft, 2004.

Alfonso, Ganymede. *The Morphed Cousin: Edward and the Many Roles of the Poetic Supporting Character*. New York: Athelstan, 1963.

Aristotle. *The Complete Works of Aristotle*. Edited by Jonathan Barnes. 2 vols. Princeton: Princeton University Press, 1984.

Armitage, Simon, trans. *The Death of Arthur: A New Verse Translation*. New York: Norton, 2012.

———, trans. *Sir Gawain and the Green Knight*. New York: Norton, 2007.

Armstrong, Karen. *Fields of Blood: Religion and the History of Violence*. New York: Knopf, 2014.

———. *A History of God: The 4,000-Year Quest of Judaism, Christianity, and Islam*. New York: Ballantine, 1993.

Asad, Talal. *Formations of the Secular: Christianity, Islam, and Modernity*. Stanford: Stanford University Press, 2003.

———. *Genealogies of Religion: Discipline and Reasons of Power in Christianity and Islam*. Baltimore: Johns Hopkins University Press, 1993.

Aslan, Reza. *Zealot: The Life and Times of Jesus of Nazareth*. New York: Random House, 2014.

Augustine. *Concerning the City of God Against the Pagans*. Translated by Henry Bettenson. New York: Penguin, 1972.

———. *Confessions*. Translated by Henry Chadwick. Oxford: Oxford University Press, 1991.

Aurelius, Marcus. *Meditations*. Translated by Martin Hammond. New York: Penguins Classics, 2006.

Bibliography

Baumgartner, Noel. "Is Crispin Disloyal to Alfred? *Sigurd's Lament* and the Role of Power." *Foucault and Friends* 12 (2001) 23–56.

Bayard, Pierre. "Anticipatory Plagiarism." Translated by Jeffrey Mehlman. *New Literary History* 44 (2013) 231–50.

Benson, Larry D., ed. and trans. "The Date of the Alliterative *Morte Arthure*." In *Medieval Studies in Honour of Lillian Herlands Hornstein*, edited by Jess Bessinger and Robert K. Raymo, 19–40. New York: New York University Press, 1976.

———, ed. *King Arthur's Death: The Middle English Stanzaic Morte Arthur and Alliterative Morte Arthure*. Revised by Edward E. Foster. Kalamazoo, MI: Medieval Institute, 1994.

Biguenet, John, and Rainer Schulte, ed. *The Craft of Translation*. Chicago: University of Chicago Press, 1992.

Bird, Michael F., et al. *How God Became Jesus: The Real Origins of Belief in Jesus' Divine Nature—A Response to Bart D. Ehrman*. Grand Rapids: Zondervan, 2014.

Blomberg, Craig L. *The Historical Reliability of the Gospels*. Downers Grove: InterVarsity, 1987.

Boileau-Despréaux, Nicolas. "The Art of Poetry." In *Critical Theory since Plato*, edited by Hazard Adams, 241–52. Rev. ed. New York: Harcourt, 1992.

Bombadil, Gerard V. "Sigurd's Choice." *Literary Choice and Character* 4 (2012) 56–90.

Borg, Marcus J. *Jesus: Uncovering the Life, Teachings, and Relevance of a Religious Revolutionary*. New York: HarperOne, 2008.

Boron, Malory L. *Sigurd's Madness*. Boston: Wipf and Boff, 2008.

Braidotti, Rosi. *The Posthuman*. Cambridge: Polity, 2013.

Bredehoft, Thomas A. *Early English Metre*. Toronto: University of Toronto Press, 2005.

Brogan, T. V. F. "Bob and Wheel." In *The New Princeton Encyclopedia of Poetry and Poetics*, edited by Alex Preminger and T. V. F. Brogan. Princeton: Princeton University Press, 1993.

Brown, Cynthia Stokes. *Big History: From the Big Bang to the Present*. New York: New Press, 2007.

Bulfinch, Thomas. *Bulfinch's Mythology*. New York: Gramercy, 1979.

Bulgakov, Mikhail. *The Master and Margarita*. Translated by Diana Burgin and Katherine Tiernan O'Conner. New York: Vintage, 1997.

Bumburry, Heather V. "The Slaves We Once Owned." *Journal of Oppression and Injustice* 1 (2011) 43–86.

Byock, Jesse L., trans. *The Saga of the Volsungs*. New York: Penguin Classics, 2000.

Cable, Thomas. *The English Alliterative Tradition*. Philadelphia: University of Pennsylvania Press, 1991.

Caesar, Michael. *Umberto Eco: Philosophy and the Work of Fiction*. Cambridge: Polity, 1999.

Bibliography

Cavendish, Margaret. *The Blazing World*. In *Paper Bodies: A Margaret Cavendish Reader*, edited by Sylvia Bowerbank and Sara Mendelson. Peterborough, ON: Broadview Literary, 2000.

Casio, Eaton. *Time Is Floating*. Jacksonville: Clockwork, 1992.

Chaff, Lord Ramsey. "An Exploration into Anglach's Gate." *Journal of English Studies* 34 (2006) 34–78.

Chandler, Daniel. *Semiotics: The Basics*. 2nd ed. New York: Routledge, 2007.

Chesterton, G. K. *The Ballad of the White Horse*. New York: Dover, 2010.

Chism, Christine. *Alliterative Revivals*. Philadelphia: University of Pennsylvania Press, 2002.

Christian, David, et al. *Big History: Between Nothing and Everything*. New York: McGraw-Hill, 2013.

Cicero, Marcus Tullius. *On Duties*. Edited by M. T. Griffin and E. M. Atkins. Cambridge: Cambridge University Press, 1991.

Cover, Jennifer Grouling. *The Creation of Narrative in Tabletop Role-Playing Games*. Jefferson, NC: McFarland, 2010.

Crantzi, Herald W. *In the Arms of Tyranny We Rise*. Portland: Hawthorne, 2014.

Crossan, John Dominic. *The Birth of Christianity*. New York: HarperCollins, 1999.

———. *The Dark Interval: Towards a Theology of Story*. Farmington, MN: Polebridge, 1988.

———. *The Historical Jesus: The Life of a Mediterranean Jewish Peasant*. New York: HarperCollins, 1992.

———. *The Power of Parable: How Fiction by Jesus Became Fiction about Jesus*. New York: HarperCollins, 2012.

Cumbrinar, Reginald E. *Life of the Assassin: Sigurd Amongst Other Tales*. Rome: Ribald, 1973.

Curtius, E. R. *European Literature and the Latin Middle Ages*. Translated by Willard R. Trask. New York: Routledge, 1953.

Danielson, Dennis Richard, ed. *The Book of the Cosmos: Imagining the Universe from Heraclitus to Hawking*. Cambridge: Basic Books, 2002.

Dante. *The Divine Comedy*. Translated by Allen Mandelbaum. New York: Vintage Classic, 2013.

Darling, Wendy. *The Problem with Perspective: A Journey of Boyhood*. London: Neverland, 1976.

Demarco, Patricia. "An Arthur for the Ricardian Age: Crown, Nobility, and the Alliterative *Morte Arthure*." *Speculum* 80 (2005) 464–93.

Dickson, Jacoby Q. *The Blood of the Guilty*. Topeka: Washburn, 2007.

Dostoevsky, Fyodor. *The Brothers Karamazov*. Translated by Richard Pevear and Larissa Volokhonsky. New York: Farrar, Straus and Giroux, 2002.

Durkheim, Émile. *The Elementary Forms of Religious Life*. Translated by Carol Cosman. Oxford: Oxford University Press, 2001.

Dyson, Rebecca L. *Art, Posey, and the Magnificent in Elaean Culture*. Seattle: RainSoaked, 1976.

Eco, Umberto. *Baudolino: A Novel*. Translated by William Weaver. New York: Harcourt, 2000.

———. *The Book of Legendary Lands*. Translated by Alastair McEwen. New York: Rizzoli Ex Libris, 2013.

———. *Inventing the Enemy*. Translated by Richard Dixon. New York: Houghton Mifflin, 2011.

———. *The Name of the Rose*. Translated by William Weaver. New York: Harvest, 1994.

———. *The Prague Cemetery*. Translated by Richard Dixon. New York: Houghton Mifflin, 2011.

———. *The Role of the Reader: Explorations in the Semiotics of Texts*. Bloomington: Indiana University Press, 1984.

———. *Semiotics and the Philosophy of Language*. Bloomington: Indiana University Press, 1986.

———. *A Theory of Semiotics*. Bloomington: Indiana University Press, 1979.

Eco, Umberto, and Carlo Maria Martini. *Belief or Nonbelief?* Translated by Minna Proctor. New York: Arcade, 2000.

Eddison, E. R. *The Worm Ouroboros*. New York: Ballantine, 1976.

Edmundson, Mark. *Why Read?* New York: Bloomsbury, 2004.

Ehrman, Bart D. *How Jesus Became God: The Exaltation of a Jewish Preacher from Galilee*. New York: HarperOne, 2014.

Eliot, T. S. "Tradition and the Individual Talent." In *Selected Prose of T. S. Elliot*, edited by Frank Kermode, 37–44. New York: Ferrar, Straus, and Giroux, 1975.

Fanon, Frantz. *Black Skin, White Masks*. Translated by Richard Philcox. New York: Grove, 2008.

———. *The Wretched of the Earth*. Translated by Richard Philcox. New York: Grove, 2005.

Foucault, Michel. *The Archaeology of Knowledge*. New York: Vintage, 1982.

———. *Discipline and Punish: The Birth of the Prison*. Translated by Alan Sheridan. New York: Penguin, 1977.

Fuligin, Severian. *Terminus Est: The Sword and the Harbinger*. New York: Citadel, 2005.

Fulk, Robert D. *A History of Old English Meter*. Philadelphia: University of Pennsylvania Press, 1992.

Gamgee, Oleander. *With the Sun We'll Rise Only to Die*. Southampton: UK & UK, 2014.

Gandhi, Mohandas Karamchand. *An Autobiography: The Story of My Experiments with Truth*. Translated by Mahadev Desai. Boston: Beacon, 1993.

Gardner, John. *The Alliterative Morte Arthure, The Owl and the Nightingale, and Five Other Middle English Poems in a Modernized Version, with Comments on the Poems*. Carbondale: Southern Illinois University Press, 1973.

Geertz, Clifford. *The Interpretation of Cultures*. New York: Basic Books, 1973.

Bibliography

Genette, Gérard. *Palimpsests: Literature in the Second Degree.* Translated by Channa Newman and Claude Doubinsky. Lincoln: University of Nebraska Press, 1997.

Gennep, Arnold van. *The Rites of Passage.* Translated by Monika B. Vizedom and Gabrielle L. Caffee. Chicago: University of Chicago Press, 1960.

Geoffrey, Lord Albion Darnell. *Propaganda as a Poetic Device.* Oxford: Oxford University Press, 2010.

Gleiser, Marcelo. *The Island of Knowledge: The Limits of Science and the Search for Meaning.* New York: Basic Books, 2014.

———. *A Tear at the Edge of Creation: A Radical New Vision for Life in an Imperfect Universe.* New York: Free Press, 2010.

Godden, Malcolm R. "Literary Language." In *The Cambridge History of the English Language,* edited by Richard M. Hogg, 1:490–535. Cambridge: Cambridge University Press, 1992.

Goering, Nelson. "*The Fall of Arthur* and *The Legend of Sigurd and Gudrún*: A Metrical Review of Three Modern English Alliterative Poems." *Journal of Inkling Studies* 5 (2015) 1–54.

Göller, Karl Heinz, ed. *The Alliterative Morte Arthure: A Reassessment of the Poem.* Cambridge: D. S. Brewer, 1981.

Goodson, Jack. "A Hound Is a Hound." *I Got This Quarterly* 7 (1932) 231–560.

Greene, Brian. *The Elegant Universe: Superstrings, Hidden Dimensions, and the Quest for the Ultimate Theory.* New York: Norton, 2010.

———. *The Fabric of the Cosmos: Space, Time, and the Texture of Reality.* New York: Norton, 2005.

———. *The Hidden Reality: Parallel Universes and the Deep Laws of the Cosmos.* New York: Norton, 2011.

Hallyn, Fernand. *The Poetic Structure of the World: Copernicus and Kepler.* Translated by Donald M. Leslie. Brooklyn: Zone, 1993.

Hamilton, Edith. *Mythology.* New York: Little, Brown, 1998.

Harper, Johnson. *Cosmology and Its Import.* Lindsborg: Bethany, 2002.

Harriman, Jessica R. "The Gods at Play and Dying." *Spectacular* 12 (2005) 67–89.

Harrist, Josiah. "An Intro to Tabletop Gaming as Ritual." *Kill Screen,* March 28, 2016. Online: https://killscreen.com/articles/an-intro-to-tabletop-gaming-as-a-ritual/.

Hatto, A. T., trans. *The Nibelungenlied.* New York: Penguin Classics, 1965.

Heaney, Seamus. *Beowulf: A New Verse Translation.* New York: Norton, 2001.

———. *Sweeny Astray: A Version from the Irish.* New York: Farrar, Straus and Giroux, 1983.

Hedges, Chris. *War Is a Force That Gives Us Meaning.* New York: Anchor, 2002.

Helvig, Karl H. *The Royal Court in Poetics.* Northfield: Olaf, 2005.

Herbrechter, Stefan. *Posthumanism: A Critical Analysis.* London: Bloomsbury, 2013.

Hermans, Hubert J., and Els Hermans-Jansen. "Dialogical Processes and Development of the Self." In *Handbook of Developmental Psychology*, edited by Jaan Valsiner and Kevin J. Connolly. London: Sage, 2003.

Hobson, Alistair M. *Through the Window of Poetry*. Dublin: Guinn Dough, 1952.

Homer. *The Iliad*. Translated by Robert Fagles. New York: Penguin, 1990.

————. *The Odyssey*. Translated by Robert Fagles. New York: Penguin, 1997.

Hoopes, James. *Peirce on Signs: Writings on Semiotic by Charles Sanders Peirce*. Chapel Hill: University of North Carolina Press, 1991.

Howe, Huon W. "Weakness as Death." *Sigurd Studies* 9 (2007) 341–67.

Hugo, Victor. *Les Misérables*. Translated by Norman Denny. New York: Penguin, 1982.

Hunt, Laird Z. *A Crocus for Your Thoughts*. Portland: Powell's, 1993.

Hurtlock, Spense Q., ed. *The Encyclopedia of Psychoanalysis and the Sigurd Complex*. Brentwood: Freud, 2006.

Jameson, Fredric. *A Singular Modernity: Essays on the Ontology of the Present*. New York: Verso, 2002.

Jewett, Robert. *Romans: A Commentary*. Minneapolis: Fortress, 2006.

Jones, Gwyn, and Thomas Jones, trans. *The Mabinogion*. London: Everyman Library, 1993.

Jorgenson, Andrew. *Of Gods and Men: A History of Criticism in the Poetry of Life and Death*. Minneapolis: Baldr, 2014.

Kaeuper, Richard W. *Chivalry and Violence in Medieval Europe*. Oxford: Oxford University Press, 1999.

————. *Holy Warriors: The Religious Ideology of Chivalry*. Philadelphia: University of Pennsylvania Press, 2009.

Kay, Gavriel Kay. *The Fionavar Tapestry*. New York: EOS, 1985.

————. *The Lions of Al-Rassan*. New York: Harper, 2005.

————. *Lord of Emperors*. New York: EOS, 2001.

————. *Sailing to Sarantium*. New York: EOS, 1998.

Kazantzakis, Nikos. *The Last Temptation of Christ*. Translated by P. A. Bien. New York: Simon & Schuster, 1960.

Krishna, Valerie. *The Alliterative "Morte Arthure."* Lanham, MD: University Press of America, 1983.

Kristeva, Julia. *Desire in Language: A Semiotic Approach to Literature and Art*. New York: Columbia University Press, 1980.

Lacan, Jacques. *Écrits*. Translated by Bruck Fink in collaboration with Héloïse Fink and Russell Grigg. New York: Norton, 2007.

Landroval, Judith X. *The Loved and the Lover in Early Modern Poetry*. London: Warwick, 1999.

Langland, William. *Piers Plowman*. Edited by Elizabeth Robertson and Stephen H. A. Shepherd. New York: Norton, 2006.

Lanthny, Acre A. *Laments and Laments: Sigrud and Genre*. Boston: Macabre, 2012.

Larrington, Carolyne, trans. *The Poetic Edda*. Oxford: Oxford University Press, 2009.

Lawson, E. Thomas. "Cognition." In *Guide to the Study of Religion*, edited by Willi Braun and Russell T. McCutcheon. London: Cassell, 2000.

Lee, Ryan Peter. *Hamlet Sheared*. London: Bard, 2004.

Lewis, C. S. *The Discarded Image: An Introduction to Medieval and Renaissance Literature*. Cambridge: Cambridge University Press, 1994.

———. *Till We Have Faces: A Myth Retold*. New York: Harvest, 1956.

Lima, Adrian R. "The Lost Gifts of Beowulf Found in Avalonia." *Anglo-Saxon Artifacts* 3 (2001) 34–89.

Lönnrot, Elias. *The Kalevala*. Translated by Keith Bosley. Oxford: Oxford University Press, 2008.

Lucan. *Pharsalia*. Translated by Jane Wilson Joyce. Ithaca: Cornell University Press, 1993.

Lucretius. *De Rerum Natura (The Nature of Things)*. Translated by David R. Slavitt. Berkeley: University of California Press, 2008.

Mabeuf, M. *The Flora of the Environs of Cauteretz*. Paris: Hugo, 2003.

Macavoy, Lucinda W. *A Cousin for a Queen*. Austin: University of Texas Press, 1989.

Magnusson, Arn. *Jüt and His Country*. Reykjavík: Viking, 1995.

———. "Valhöll in the Life of a God." *Journal of Norse Studies* 76 (1994) 234–58.

Malory, Thomas. *Le Morte Darthur*. New York: Norton, 2003.

———. *Malory: Complete Works*. Edited by Eugene Vinaver. Oxford: Oxford University Press, 1971.

Mandela, Nelson. *Long Walk to Freedom: The Autobiography of Nelson Mandela*. Boston: Little, Brown, 1994.

Mandry, Zia. "Wives and Their Authors." *Feminine Literature* 17 (2011) 156–78.

Marin, Brendan H. "Lords of War and Play." *War Studies* 89 (2004) 98–143.

Marlow, Jessica. *The Curse and Its Properties*. Jacksonville: Florida, 1984.

Masterson, Edward R. "The Canceling of Fate." *Journal for Linguistic Poetry* 11 (1969) 112–43.

Meloy, Colin. *Wildwood*. The Wildwood Chronicles, Book 1. New York: HarperCollins, 2011.

Middleton, Darren J. N. *Broken Hallelujah: Nikos Kazantzakis and Christian Theology*. Lanham, MD: Lexington, 2006.

———, ed. *God, Literature, and Process Thought*. Burlington, VT: Ashgate, 2002.

———. *Novel Theology: Nikos Kazantzakis's Encounter with Whiteheadian Process Theism*. Macon, GA: Mercer University Press, 2000.

———. *Theology after Reading: Christian Imagination and the Power of Fiction*. Waco: Baylor University Press, 2008.

Milton, John. *Paradise Lost*. Edited by Alastair Fowler. Rev. ed. New York: Routledge, 2007.

Mitchell, Stephen. *Gilgamesh: A New English Version*. New York: Atria, 2006.

Moore, Edward C., ed. *Charles S. Peirce: The Essential Writings*. New York: Prometheus, 1998.

Morris, William. *The House of the Wolfings*. Coventry: Longmans, Green, 1904.

———. *The Roots of the Mountain*. Coventry: Longmans, Green, 1896.

———. *The Story of Gunnlaug the Worm-Tongue and Raven the Skald*. Coventry: Longmans, Green, 1875.

———. *The Story of Sigurd the Volsung and the Fall of the Niblungs*. Coventry: Longmans, Green, 1904.

———. *The Tale of Beowulf Sometime King of the Folk of the Weder Geats*. Coventry: Longmans, Green, 1895.

———. *The Water of the Wondrous Isles*. Coventry: Longmans, Green, 1907.

———. *The Well at the World's End*. Coventry: Longmans, Green, 1896.

———. *The Wood beyond the World*. Coventry: Longmans, Green, 1894.

Motte, Warren F., Jr., trans. and ed. *Oulipo: A Primer of Potential Literature*. Lincoln: University of Nebraska Press, 1986.

Mulisch, Harry. *The Discovery of Heaven*. Translated by Paul Vincent. New York: Penguin, 2011.

Munroe, Terry. *The Ides of Sigurd*. Aberdeen: Aberdeen, 1992.

Nievergelt, Marco. "Conquest, Crusade and Pilgrimage: The Alliterative *Morte Arthure* in Its Late Ricardian Crusading Context." *Arthuriana* 20 (2010) 89–116.

Olsen, Alexandra H., ed. *Poems and Prose from the Old English*. Translated by Burton Raffle. New Haven: Yale University Press, 1998.

Orsi, Robert A. *Between Heaven and Earth: The Religious Worlds People Make and the Scholars Who Study Them*. Princeton: Princeton University Press, 2006.

Ouera, Mandel. "Life in Oppressive Regimes." *Fanon Studies* 6 (2003) 12–27.

Ovid. *Metamorphoses*. Translated by Charles Martin. New York: Norton, 2004.

———. *Metamorphoses*. Translated by A. D. Melville. Oxford: Oxford University Press, 2009.

Patterson, Lee. *Negotiating the Past: The Historical Understanding of Medieval Literature*. Madison: University of Wisconsin Press, 1987.

Peters, Benjamin John. *On the Matter of Texts*. Cresthill: Interior, 2017.

———. *Through All the Plain*. Eugene, OR: Cascade, 2013.

Peters, Hawthorne Basil. *Distention and Its Many Objects: A Journey into Texts and Their Worlds, or Bloom*. Dorning: Confessions, 1963.

———. *Finley: A Story of the Twelve Kingdoms, Taken from, Tales of Ages Gone By, A History of Elaea in Three Volumes*. Vol. 5. Seaboard: Fiction, 2013.

———. *Greer: A Story of the Twelve Kingdoms, Taken from, Tales of Ages Gone By, A History of Elaea in Three Volumes*. Vol. 6-II. Seaboard: Fiction, 2014.

———. *Regan: A Story of the Twelve Kingdoms, Taken from, Tales of Ages Gone By, A History of Elaea in Three Volumes*. Vol. 4. Seaboard: Fiction, 2012.

———. *Religion in the Life of Sigurd*. Oxford: Oxford University Press, 1999.

Peters, Natasha Vukovich. *Sexism in Alliterative Verse: The Role of Gender in Poetry*. Oxford: Oxford University Press, 2010.

———. *Women at Play both Deadly and Dreadful.* Oxford: Oxford University Press, 2008.

Peters, Wallace Walker. *Notes and Letters: A Life Written.* Edited by Hawthorne Basil Peters. Oxford: Oxford University Press, 1973.

Pettit, Holly. "The Snows of Sigurd." *Alliterative Quarterly* 47 (2007) 87–112.

Piuma, Chris. "Anticipatory Plagiarism and the *ex post facto*-Garde." *Postmedieval: A Journal of Medieval Cultural Studies* 4 (2013) 305–9.

Plato. *Plato: Complete Works.* Edited by John M. Cooper. Indianapolis: Hackett, 2007.

Plotinus. *The Enneads.* Translated by Stephen MacKenna. New York: Penguin, 1991.

Pope Francis. *Evangelii Gaudium.* Apostolic Exhortation on the Proclamation of the Gospel in Today's World. Rome: Vatican, 2013.

Quenya, Laura M. *When the Cock Crows in Sigurd.* London: Press of the Free, 2003.

Qumbestro, Sylvano. *War and Narrative.* Rome: Vatican, 1923.

Raffel, Burton. *The Art of Translating Poetry.* University Park: Penn State University Press, 1988.

———. *The Art of Translating Prose.* University Park: Penn State University Press, 1994.

Renie, Ernst K. *Eustace the Traitor.* New York: Wingie, 2002.

Reuel, Ronald. *The Bonds of Brotherhood and Family in Elaean Life and Culture.* Downtown: Abbey, 1957.

Ringler, Dick. *Beowulf: A New Translation for Oral Delivery.* Indianapolis: Hackett, 2007.

Robinson, Marilynne. *Gilead: A Novel.* New York: Picador, 2004.

Rothfuss, Patrick. *The Name of the Wind.* New York: DAW Books, 2008.

Rubenstein, Mary-Jane. *Worlds without End: The Many Lives of the Multiverse.* New York: Columbia University Press, 2014.

Russell, Mary Doria. *The Sparrow: A Novel.* New York: Ballantine, 1997.

Russom, Geoffrey. *Beowulf and Old Germanic Metre.* Cambridge: Cambridge University Press, 1998.

Said, Edward W. *Orientalism.* New York: Vintage, 1979.

Sartre, Jean-Paul. "Existentialism." In *From Modernism to Postmodernism: An Anthology,* edited by Lawrence E. Cahoone, 259–73. Oxford: Blackwell, 1996.

Saussure, Ferdinand de. *Course in General Linguistics.* Edited by Charles Bally and Albert Sechehaye with the collaboration of Albert Riedlinger. Translated by Roy Harris. LaSalle, IL: Open Court, 1998.

Sayers, Dorothy L., trans. *The Song of Roland.* New York: Penguin, 1957.

Schulte, Rainer, and John Biguenet, eds. *Theories of Translation: An Anthology of Essays from Dryden to Derrida.* Chicago: University of Chicago Press, 1992.

Seligman, Adam B., et al. *Ritual and Its Consequences.* Oxford: Oxford University Press, 2008.